Growing Up in Italy in a Time of War

Gioietta Vitale

PROSPECTA PRESS

Copyright © 2012 by Gioietta Vitale

Paperback ISBN 978-1-935212-69-0
E-book ISBN 978-1-935212-58-4

Cover design by Barbara Aronica-Buck

All rights reserved. No portion of this book may be reproduced in any fashion, including print, facsimile, or electronic, or by any method yet to be developed, without the express written permission of the publisher.

Published by
Prospecta Press
P.O. Box 3131
Westport, CT 06880
(203) 454-4454
www.prospectapress.com

Published May 2012

I dedicate this book with love to my two sons, Raffaele and Alessandro, and their beautiful children, Nicole, Julia, Sara, Elisa, Sabina, Peter and Lavinia

INTRODUCTION

The wonderful reality is that there is no escape. It is our maturity which keeps us linked to our past like prisoners. Sometimes we tend not to remember, and we lock up our memories in the most remote place in our brain cells. Memories fill up our minds, together with our sensations, images, and impulses. I am determined to dedicate my time to recalling the years of my childhood before and during World War II. It seems ages since my childhood in Italy. In my memory, however, it feels like yesterday. Good and bad memories are as vivid as ever, imprinted on my mind. It is amazing how quickly they come back. All it takes to make them click into focus is a smell, a sound, a snapshot, a sensation . . . feelings, smells, colors, words of the past are all recorded in our memory and will never leave us. They are part of us, who we are, even if we do not realize it. The past as well as the present will mold the future.

I will try to capture those images of everyday life that are kept locked in my memory, not only for my personal satisfaction, but for my children and grandchildren, so that they may learn how life used to be. Everything changes in the span of one lifetime, some for the better, some for the worse. However, memories, like knowledge, cannot be taken away from you.

So here are my memories, recaptured for those who are curious to know how life was in Italy before, during, and after the Second World War.

Chapter 1

June 10th, 1940. It is a bright, sunny day in our garden in Milan. Three of us children are playing in the so-called swimming pool. Really it is just a big fountain shaped like a half moon. We live in a big house surrounded by a lot of attention and love. My family consists of four girls and two boys: Giana, Grazia nicknamed Lalla, myself, Gabriella nicknamed Baby, and the two boys, Dominic and Mario Jr. The eldest, Giana, was fifteen when she was struck by a severe case of pneumonia. Unfortunately, at that time in our country there was nothing available to cure her, not even sulfonamide. She left us, creating a big void in our lives.

The air is filled with our happy, garrulous screams. Suddenly the entrance to the garden opens and a horse cabby enters. This appearance makes a commotion in our group. We all run to greet Father, who is descending from the cab. He is a handsome gentleman, smiling and embracing us one by one. Lalla is with him. Father tells us to dry off and hurry inside the house to listen to the radio. Benito Mussolini, our Duce, is delivering a speech in which he will announce his decision about whether or not to go to war. I'm a little girl, but I feel how crucial this is for all of us. A sudden, vague malaise grips my stomach, and I wrap the dry towel around my wet body as tightly as I can.

Quickly, and without a word, we rush into the house to listen to Mussolini's speech, which was already underway. The high pitch of his voice fills the living room, hits the ceiling, and echoes back to us. We children are intimidated by the tone of Mussolini's voice. We gather together and sit on the marble floor, smooth and cool. Mussolini's speech is long and noisy. The audience, I believe, in Piazza Venezia in Rome, interrupts at each sentence screaming "DUCE DUCE DUCE DUCE" in unison.

I am bored. I look at the sunlight coming in through the tall window overlooking a spacious terrace. It's where our sister Lalla often roller-skates with her best friend Pupina, each of them with a pillow fastened to their buttocks. We always watch them in astonishment and giggle.

I am awakened from my thoughts by the screaming of "WAR WAR WAR DUCE DUCE." I'm frightened—I don't know what is happening. I look at Father, his head gently bent, holding Mother's hand. The radio is crackling, and the sound invades our living room. The oceanic audience of Piazza Venezia is in delirium, clapping and screaming and singing "DUCE DUCE DUCE." It is a scary world, and to me it seems to be going mad.

Father slowly shuts off the radio. No one is moving, and no word is uttered. An enormous silence embraces us.

I do not really know what war means, but I do know it is a bad choice. I don't have a clear understanding, but I'm feeling sad and uneasy.

Father is now talking to Mother, and we're listening. "I am really surprised," Daddy says. "Just yesterday I was in Finale Ligure and had dinner at the Miramare restaurant where I met a couple of Frenchmen and started a conversation with them. They told me they were pilots and had come to pick up some airplanes manufactured by the local Piaggio plant for the French Government." Mother and Father agree that it's a bizarre situation.

We resume our swimming. I am confused. I do not feel happy anymore. I want to go back to before Mussolini's speech; his raucous voice is echoing in my head. I am asking myself, in rage, "how can he do this? He is out of his silly mind and all those people cheering him! How could he do that? What is going to happen next?" I don't feel like swimming or playing. I am mad, and my sister Baby doesn't understand my mood. She looks at me and says, "What's the matter with you now?"

The same night we wake up at the sound of sirens breaking the silence of the warm, peaceful summer night. The grown-ups urge us to get up, dress, and follow them to the bomb shelter. We do not understand; we scream, cry and beg the grown-ups to leave us alone. They carry the little ones in their arms and drag the older ones along. Luckily the bomb shelter is just one block away from us. The shelter is located in the basement of the Isotta Fraschini factory . . . not a safe place to take refuge from an air raid. This factory is one of the leading Italian airplane manufacturers. I see shining flashes in the dark sky. I hear the sound of airplanes and ambulance sirens cruising the city, the sound of bombs hitting the buildings. I am scared, and I run as fast as possible along with the others. We do not know it, but we are very lucky that no shells hit our neighborhood.

The next morning when we wake up we see luggage ready, and we notice a Red Cross ambulance parked in our driveway. Mother has decided that we have to evacuate from the city as soon as we can, and indeed the use of an ambulance is the fastest and only possible way. Cars have been banned for private use. No gasoline is available.

We children are very excited and literally speechless. No one has to tell us to get dressed and go downstairs for breakfast. We consume it without lifting an eye, and when we're done we race to take our seats in the ambulance, looking at each other, puzzled. Around us is a great commotion: luggage brought into the vehicle, bags, garment holders, boxes and the like. Father, who I guess is not going to the office yet, is giving orders left and right, and I see his head peeping in the back of the ambulance. He seems quite surprised to see all of us sitting in silence. He smiles to us and tells the driver to take off.

We start our journey. Mother is sitting in the front with the driver, in order to direct him. We're going down the driveway. I look through the back window of the ambulance, which is quite wide, and I see our house getting smaller and smaller and suddenly it is no more. I hear Mother say we are going to Ghiffa, a pleasant, sleepy village on Lake Maggiore.

Sitting with us in the ambulance is our nanny, Ernesta. The fact that she is among us doesn't please us children at all. The occasion, however, is so unusual that we do not pay any attention to her. Ernesta is not the most pleasant person to be with. She is always scolding us, often with no reason, and she adores her power over us and exercises it with gusto. Just my luck, she is sitting in front of me. She is wearing a light coat, grayish in color, on top of her white uniform. I am sure Mother gave her this coat; it is quite an elegant outfit. Ernesta's black hair is pulled back in a chignon on top of her short, flabby neck. Her hair is so tight that her eyeballs are literally popping out of their sockets. Her complexion is grayish-white like her coat, and she looks straight at me with no expression. I try to avoid meeting her eyes and direct my attention to the landscape outside.

It's taking some time before we reach the suburbs. On both sides of the road are rows of buildings of the same height and shape. These tenements have been built by Mussolini to house the people who came to the city from the country to work in the various industries. These houses are called *case popolari*. Crawling bikes, trams, municipal and commuter buses, and pedestrians are coming and going into and out of the city. So much is going on that my head is spinning.

And yet I am very taken by this new environment. I keep quiet and attentive, and soon the city traffic fades away. Yellow fields splashed by delicate red poppies catch my eye. The golden crop is ready to be harvested. The fields are shining under the strong June sun. They remind me of paintings I saw in a French art book called *The Impressionists*. It is so beautiful that I am enchanted and speechless.

Now the road is almost empty, with only a few bikes and rural horse-driven carts carrying piles of hay marching literally in the middle of the road. The one in front of us doesn't move; I am sure the peasant at the helm is napping away; the horse without guidance goes zigzagging from one side of the road to the other. Our driver is furious. He starts screaming at the top of his lungs while sounding the car's horn at full blast. Mother tries to calm him down. All of us start screaming as well to the poor sleepy peasant. Ernesta wakes up from her lethargy. "Stop this nonsense at once!" she yells.

The cart moves to the right side of the street, and our driver can pass him.

We are going through a village now. The driver is slowing down the vehicle once again. The inhabitants of this village mostly stroll in the middle of the main road carrying baskets full of produce. In all probability it is market day. Church bells are ringing announcing midday. I am enchanted by the clear sound of the bells which fill the air with their magic.

The atmosphere is changing dramatically. Everything is still, no more horse-driven carts, no bikes, no people, just the sun-drenched white asphalt of the road in front of us. It is lunch time. Our driver is delighted to be able to keep up a decent speed. I guess he, like us, is longing to get to our destination.

We are getting closer to the lake now. No more golden fields, no more rural villages, but a narrow winding road takes us "*au bord du lac.*" I open the car window next to my seat, and the smell of water fills my nostrils. It feels good, fresh, invigorating.

Many old patrician villas sunken in deep green patches surrounded by secular trees and ravishing gardens plaster the hillside next to the road. We are getting close to our final destination at last. I am excited and impatient, but mostly my fellow passengers are still dozing away. The ambulance makes a sharp turn into the Ghiffa Grand Hotel driveway. As soon as the engine stops, we are out of the car.

I am quite impressed by the hotel. Its plain façade has large, ornate stone windows with a floral design which give to the building a solid as well as a gentle look. Two rather handsome concierges and a couple of porters are waiting for us. I guess Father has announced our unusual arrival by ambulance. We assemble in front of the reception desk, and after Mother finishes the registrations, we follow the pompous hotel manager who is escorting us to our designated rooms. My sister Baby and I share the same room. We are pleased; the room is spacious and the window faces the lake, which is shining under the strong June afternoon sun. I am glad it is the month of June and it is a bright, sunny day. The lake can be pretty depressing when it is raining or the sky is overcast. A melancholic feeling grips me when that happens.

As soon as the porter puts our luggage on the rack located under the tall window and leaves, my sister and I start unpacking. Ernesta appears at the door telling us to wash up and follow her to the dining room for lunch. With all the excitement I am not hungry, but we have to follow her anyway.

After lunch we are allowed to roam through the park that surrounds the hotel. The place is quite spacious; secular trees give a delicious shade to the winding path. I run until my legs hurt and I am short of breath. I sit down on the cool green grass. Slowly I lie down and look up at the blue sky. The smell of the lake is strong and penetrating—I breathe deep and let it come into my lungs. It feels good, earthy, relaxing after our trip and the bombings of last night.

At dinner I am exhausted and can barely make it through without falling asleep. I am the first one to go to bed—quite unusual for me—expecting to fall asleep right away, but my eyes are wide open. The room is not fully dark; the light of the corridor filters in. I keep looking at that narrow ray of light and listening in case someone is walking by. I am thinking about my room. I miss the familiar sounds. I miss even the song of the drunken man in the street below my bedroom window. I would have never thought I would already miss my school and my friends, even my teachers . . . all the things and people we left behind which we take for granted.

Chapter 2

In Milan I had attended a nuns' school, l'Istituto delle Suore Marcelline di Piazza Tommaseo. It was the same convent where Mother and her sisters had attended classes. Monsignor Luigi Biraghi founded this convent in 1859 and named it after Santa Marcellina, sister of St. Ambrogio, who first was Bishop of Milan (374 to 397) and then became its Patron. Biraghi was invited to join the College of Doctors of the prestigious Biblioteca Ambrosiana for his vast knowledge in philosophy and theology. The Austrian Authority supported his candidacy to this post since Monsignor Biraghi was the dean of an important seminary, and his strong liberal teaching was considered a threat to the Austrians. Milan at the time was still under the Austro-Hungarian Empire, on the verge of becoming part of the new Regno d'Italia. The Regno d'Italia was proclaimed in March of 1861 by the great statesman Count Camillo Benso di Cavour, who was running the Savoia State of Piedmont.

Milan, capital of Lombardy, was fertile country with great

agricultural resources and an industrious population, contrary to the other northern Italian Provinces, which at the time were very poor and over-populated. Milan was a lively city, with a high society, industrialists, business men, doctors, intellectuals, musicians, and politicians. In a growing bourgeois society, Milan needed institutions for higher education, especially for the young daughters of this prominent society. The Istituto delle Suore Marcelline became the place where the young minds of the Milanese society were challenged in philosophy, art, music, literature, and mathematics.

The convent was located in an exclusive residential part of the city. It was a beautiful mansion surrounded by a spacious park with secular trees . . . an oasis conducive to teaching and learning.

The nuns, le Suore Marcelline, ran the school with an iron fist, and they were very demanding academically. High grades should be kept in order to pass classes. Homework should be done after classes and before going home. The boarding students were expected to attend the Holy Mass before going to classes. I was not one of them because I lived at home and was not required to go to Mass. I liked my school, and I got along with my teachers.

Among the nuns one beautiful young lady stood out. Gossip circulated among us students about her. Apparently this young nun took the vows after an unhappy love affair. She was tall and handsome and belonged to a prominent

Milanese family. I loved the way she walked. Her posture was regal; she carried her head as though she was wearing a crown. She looked like a queen and acted like one, and I was fascinated by her. She seemed to belong to another planet. I admired her immensely, as did everybody else in my class. When she passed us on the staircase her long, wide, black skirt moved gently and left behind a delicate smell of eau de cologne. We retreated and let her go by and looked at each other with a look of complicity and excitement. There was always someone whispering new details about her unhappy romance. We never ceased to talk about her.

At school we were not compelled to dress like "Piccole Italiane," which was the Fascist dress code for school children. If you attended public school, on certain days you had to show up for class in uniform for the *adunate* (meetings.) The Fascist uniform for girls was quite pretty. It consisted of a black pleated skirt up to the knees and a white blouse. The boys' uniform consisted of black flannel shorts, a white cotton shirt, and a cap similar to the Moroccan fez, though instead of red it was black with an ornamental tassel of the same color on top.

Our school uniform was a white smock buttoned in front that we wore on top of our dresses. A couple of times I was caught wearing shorts, and when that happened I was severely reprimanded, as if I had been sinning, and was threatened with being summoned to Mother Superior's office.

The class I abhorred most was embroidering, which we had once a week. I had no patience, and I did not know how to embroider. I was restless, I would get up from my seat, talk to my friends, and the nun in charge scolded me all the time. She decided that during the embroidery class I would have to stand up at the teacher's desk in front of the whole class and read the life of a saint. This time it was the life of Santa Teresa. In the beginning I was so proud of being up there at the teacher's desk that I read loudly and clearly, and all of the students were hanging on my every word. It felt good, and I was really proud and pleased with myself and so was the nun. I saw her smiling while she was doing my work . . . the best piece of embroidering I have done in my whole life. I saw as well that my fellow students were quite surprised by my enthusiasm and kept quiet. It just happened that after a while I got bored of hearing my own voice, so I started skipping, first words then little by little full sentences and lines, to the amusement of my forced audience.

At first it was just a little giggling here and there, then plain laughter exploded and the nun lifted her head from her work, looking around trying to figure out what was going on. Then as soon as she realized I was the cause of such an outbreak she looked at me, bewildered, and started screaming, "How do you dare? Report right away to Mother Superior's office." I was stunned. I would never have expected such a reaction from such a sweet, gentle creature. I did not even try to plead for forgiveness. The sister was visibly upset.

Reporting to Mother Superior was something no one looked forward to. Slowly I proceeded toward the class door. I felt miserable. I descended the wide staircase, stopping every once in a while to delay the encounter with the supreme authority as much as possible. Suddenly I arrived at the hated door. I paused to regain my confidence and knocked. "Come in," I heard. I cautiously opened the door and saw, in the semi-obscurity of the room, Mother Superior seated at her desk reading some papers she was holding in her white, skinny hands, lit up from a small lamp on her desk. Without lifting up her head she asked, "May I help you?"

I was panicking, and I did not know what to say to her, so I just looked at her in silence. She was smiling at me, so I said "well." "Yes?" she said. "Well," I said again, "see I was supposed to read the story of Santa Theresa in class." She nodded her head, giving me a little more confidence, so I told her, "I was making the class laugh because of my skipping words of the text."

Mother Superior was not smiling anymore. Her face dropped, her eyes like two colored rocks. "This certainly is not the way to behave in front of the entire class. You do not fool around with Saints, my dear young lady." I was afraid, so I kept my head down and prayed. My punishment: to read Saint Theresa's book and write a report which should be submitted to her for review.

I left Mother Superior's room in a somber mood.

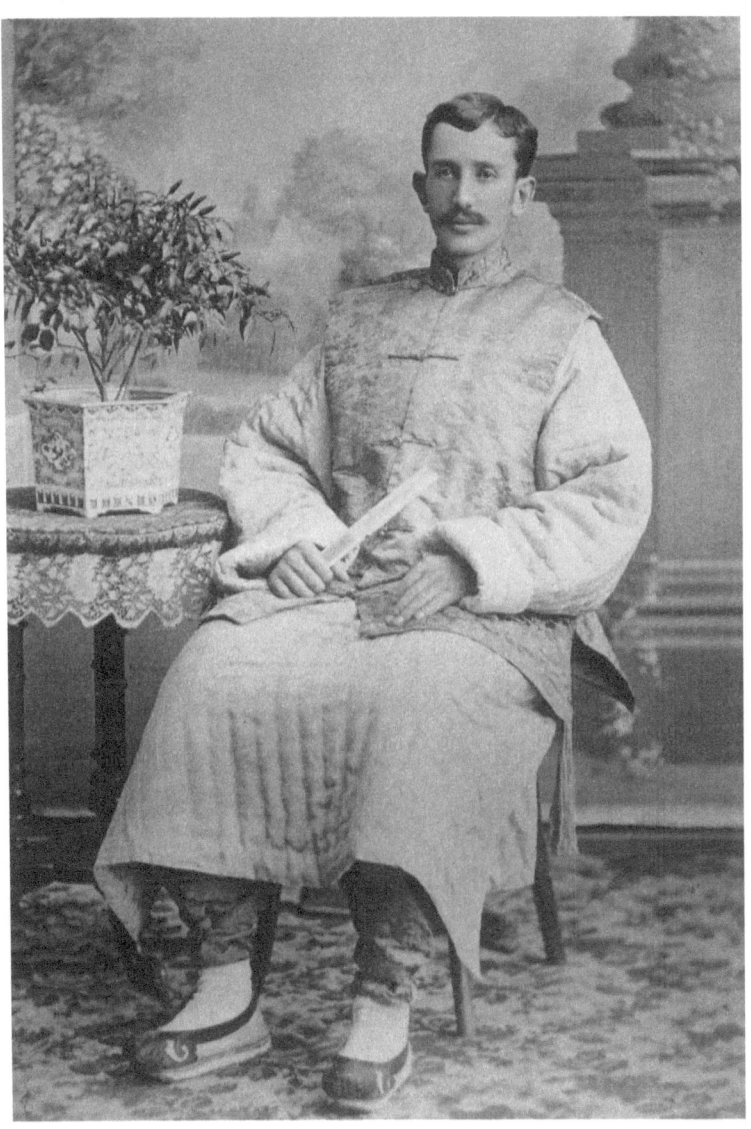

Chapter 3

Our house had been built in the year 1925 by an architect related to my mother's side of the family. He married my mother's sister, Giuseppina Castelnovo. Natale Bizzozzero was part of an architecture team who designed the International Fair in Milan in 1920, where one of its pavilions is named after him. Our villa was a three-story building made of red bricks reflecting the style of Italian architecture of its time. It was surrounded by a park of tall poplar trees and intricate alleys of shrubbery and fragrant bushes of roses. The cherry tree is the one I was most fond of. It stood in the middle of the backyard. In June, when the cherries were starting to ripen, we children spent our time climbing up the tree and filling our bellies with cherries. The garden was beautifully kept by the gardeners, the same ones who take care of the San Siro horse track close to our house. Mother's roses got special treatment. It seems horse manure is the best fertilizer for roses. I can vouch for it. Our roses were so beautiful and admired. Indeed, they were my mother's pride and joy.

The San Siro Hippodrome was not even one mile further up the road from us. Ernest Hemingway described this horse track so well in *A Farewell to Arms*. Hemingway spent several months in a Milan Hospital while recovering from an injury suffered in World War I. He was an international Red Cross ambulance driver. During his recovery period in Milan, Hemingway had a love affair with a British nurse, which unfortunately ended tragically. He spent most of his time at the horse track in San Siro, gambling and drinking—habits, I believe, he cultivated all his life.

Our villa was called "villa delle campanelle." Two bronze bells hung at the garden entrance door, the alternative to the regular electric bell. We noticed that almost every visitor who came to the house pulled the bronze bells and immediately afterwards rang the regular bell. Once in the garden you were met by a stone staircase leading to a porch, where the entrance was located. In front of the formal dining room, the kitchen occupied an ample space, with three large windows facing the back and the side of the yard. It was vociferous and animated; people went in and out constantly at any time of day or evening. It was the heart of the house, where you learned what was happening inside and outside, sometimes even before it happened.

A ringing box hung on one of the walls of the kitchen. If Mother called from the master bedroom the number one appeared on the screen, if the number two came up it meant the call came from the dining room, and so on. The kitchen was the place to be if one wanted to stay up to date with the latest gossip. Peppina the cook, who had been in our household as long as I could remember, was the queen of her castle and made sure that everyone knew it. She terrorized our young friends when they came to play with us. I felt sorry for the young and pretty new maids. I overheard Peppina saying, "believe me when these girls are so young and pretty they are only trouble, mark my words." Of course she felt threatened; she was old and not so attractive. Mother didn't want us to hang around the kitchen, but we couldn't obey her; it was so much fun and so entertaining.

To the left of the kitchen there was the so-called office, or breakfast room, and to its left the red dining room where we children consumed our meals. The *boiserie*, or paneling, of the room and the table and the long banquette were lacquered in red. It was a cheerful place. This was my favorite room in the whole house, being so informal and full of light. Here we could actually do whatever we wanted and no one would scold us. Sometimes we would play with a little soft ball and we could get away with it. After lunch in winter time, when we had finished with our homework, we would all gather in this room to play our favorite game, Monopoly. Almost in front of the red dining room there were four doors leading to the formal dining room, which was used for entertainment. During the month of May, the month dedicated to la Madonna, Mother would recite the Holy

Rosary, and everybody would gather in front of the fireplace in the formal dining room. During May in Milan the evenings get chilly, so around six p.m. the big fireplace was lit up.

The little ones would fall fast asleep in the arms of the grown-ups, lulled by the litanies "*Santa Maria prega per noi*, Saint Mary pray for us, Saint Anne pray for us . . ." I would feel my eyes getting heavy. I tried to keep them open, but before long the warmth of the fire and the rosary did the trick. Ernesta touched me and said it was bed time, wake up. I was stiff, and painfully I'd drag myself upstairs to the cold bed. The linens were so cold that they seemed wet. I'd toss a couple of times, too tired to complain and suddenly I guess I would fall asleep.

I forgot to mention that at the very end of the entrance hall there was a small, dark, cold powder room which I hated dearly. Close to it a narrow staircase led to the basement. The basement consisted of a large pool room where we were not allowed to play. Our playroom, full to capacity with toys, was where we were free to do what we wanted, and the large refrigerated room was for fur storage and other perishable goods. But the spot we children liked the most was the workshop room where Signorelli the carpenter worked. When he was not busy with housekeeping, he was busy preparing the Christmas presepio. Each year you would be surprised how many new items he added to the setting of this presepio. He built mountains, trees, bridges, and animals all in wood. The trees were painted and so were the animals. He used pieces of mirror to make the little lakes and rivers. The effect was real, the details executed to perfection.

Signorelli was a genius. I enjoyed watching him at work—in his hands a piece of wood became alive. He was not only a gifted carpenter but a terrific story-teller as well. He was our entertainer. We liked to spend the afternoon listening to his wonderful tales. When we disappeared, the grown-ups knew where to find us.

Close to the Signorelli's workshop there was the wine cellar. Father's cellar had a large selection of rare French, German, and Italian wines. When I went by, since I liked the smell of the cellar which consisted of a mixture of cork, wine, and mildew, I would put my head in and breathe deeply. The garage was on the left side of the wine cellar. This was Angiolino's kingdom: chauffer and butler factotum. Angiolino had short legs, a big bald head, crossed eyes, and smelled of grease and gasoline. He was always busy washing the cars or fixing our bicycles, often goofing around, reading the newspaper, smoking, or courting one of the younger maids. He was also a pathological liar. He was famous for being a *mangia preti* as well as a womanizer. I once overheard in the kitchen "Angiolino runs after any skirt." Go figure. I personally could not stand the sight of Angelino—it made me sick just to look at him. He looked somehow decent when he was forced to shower and wear the uniform when he drove Mother around the city or to social functions.

One flight up from the main entrance, through the pink marble staircase, were the living quarters. The first door on the right led to my sister Lalla's bedroom. It was an ample, cheerful room. The walls were covered with yellow silk tapestries, and the twin beds were covered in the same fabric. A dark wood chest of drawers sat on the floor, with a square mirror on top of it reflecting the yellow of the silk tapestry. It seemed that the sun was shining all the time. A table in front of one of the windows with a chair completed the furnishing of the room.

My sister Grazia was tall, blonde, and slender, with delicate features, intense blue eyes, and a porcelain complexion. She had a talent for drawing as well. She was going to be a painter. Lalla was going to have private classes held by the Painter Attilio Andreoli. Attilio Andreoli was part of a group of painters called Scapigliatura Milanese. He was born in Milan on April 7th, 1877 and died in 1950. He attended the Brera Academy with famous teachers like Bertini, Tallone and Bignami. Among Andreolis' paintings the "L'onomastico del Parroco" is in the permanent collection of the Galleria Civica d'Arte Moderna in Milan, while his famous big oil canvas is hanging at the Ospedale Maggiore in Milan. This painting has been praised by the art community. Many other paintings are in private galleries as well as in private collections.

Andreoli was painting a portrait of Daddy. Daddy was sitting at his desk with our brother Dominic standing beside him. This was a project which had been in the works for at least one year, if not more. Sometimes it was the artist's fault, but more often it was Daddy's. As you might have detected, he was very seldom at home. He was always at the office, on business trips. Andreoli was living with us, trying to catch a moment for Daddy to pose for his portrait. So much time had elapsed since Andreoli started painting that my brother had grown, and I had to lend my legs to finish the painting. I was flattered, but posing was not quite my favorite past time. You had to stay still all the time while Andreoli painted. For me staying still was very difficult. I would feel like scratching my left leg, then my knee, my right foot is getting numb, I am restless, all while the painter is doing his job. With a spatula he put some color on the canvas, looked at me, took away some of the color he'd used before picking a yellow gold and starting to paint my legs. I tried my best to stay still, but I kept moving, not much but enough to make the artist unhappy. Even if he doesn't say anything, I feel it.

I was amazed by how, at a stroke of Andreoli's spatula, my legs were coming alive on the canvas. What a wonderful gift to be able to paint so beautifully. I know Andreoli pretended he didn't notice that I was not staying still, but I saw him smiling under his long white beard. I realized now why he always smelled of oil and the like. He was an artist, and he sure looked like one. His long, silvery-white hair reached his neck while his long, white, curly beard fell gently in front like an embroidered bib. He wore a large-brim felt hat winter and summer and layers and layers of clothing in the winter. I am sure his house had no central heating. When Andreoli came to our house I was amazed at how long it took him to take off those layers of clothing. While painting he wore a long cream smock smeared with oil paint. He often cleaned his hand or spatula on his smock with an automatic gesture while he looked at his work. He used his hand to retouch his strokes along with the spatula. I never saw him use a brush.

"Good, good," he said, apparently happy with his work. I relaxed and became a better model. At last Father's portrait was completed, and I was no longer asked to model. I was relieved and yet sorry not to be part of this project any more.

The portrait was admired by family and friends alike. I was flattered and told everybody that my brother's legs were actually mine.

Andreoli also painted a beautiful portrait of Mother which hung on the wall in her bedroom. Mother and Father's master bedroom was close to my eldest sister's room. It was the biggest room of the house. The walls were covered with red silk brocade, as was the bed cover. The mahogany bed frame had four little columns, with *putti* on top of the two bottom ones. It was a beautiful piece of furniture which dominated the room. I loved this bed, so big, soft and comfortably inviting. Many times I tried to sneak into this amazing haven. Sometimes I succeeded, while other times I was sent back to my own bed.

Four wide windows, two facing south, led to a narrow balcony which covered the perimeter of the bedroom. The other two windows faced the garden. A Maggiolino chest of drawers decorated the wall in front of the bed, and two armchairs in each corner completed the décor of my parents' bedroom.

A door to the left of that room took you to Mother's boudoir, where a simple light green lacquered table stood in front of a large window with a chair of the same style in front of it. It was here where my mother handled her correspondence, wrote her notes, paid bills, took telephone calls, read the newspaper, and read books. It was her shelter. We were not allowed to enter without having been summoned. In this room there was a big armoire, light green lacquered like the rest of the furniture, full of Mother's beautiful, elegant clothes. Every single item was placed in order of color as well as category: all black evening gowns together, the white, soft, organdy gowns together with the silk blouses, then the linen summer dresses, and on the top shelves all the hats, one after the other in perfect color harmony.

When opening Mother's closet one knew which season it was. Often I snuck into her boudoir to look at her closet. I would grab the first garment I found and gently put my face to it, holding my breath in order to enjoy the delicate scent of the Chanel No. 5, Mother's favorite perfume. This scent lingered in the room like incense in a church. I adored it.

Mother was tall, elegant, and full of life. Her radiant smile made people happy. She had that rare gift. Her black hair was parted in the middle, and her eyes were of an intense sparkling blue color. Her name was Gemma, and she came from a family of four girls, Giuseppina, Gemma, Germana, and Gabriella, and one boy, Piero. Paolo and Giovanna Castelnovo, their parents, resided in Parabiago, a village north of Milan, and spent their lives there, except when Paolo went to China as a young man to learn the art of silk textile. In 1882, Paolo Castelnovo, my grandfather, got an offer to go to China to manage a silk filature in Shanghai. He didn't think twice—he accepted with no hesitation. Paolo was young, energetic, intelligent, and eager to learn and travel the world. It didn't matter to him that China was far away, either physically or culturally, from his native land. He sailed to China from Marseille on a French steamer on a hot August day. He started his new job at the Shanghai filature in late October, staying at his post until the three-year contract expired.

I still have the contract he signed with the Kung Pin Filature Company of Shanghai, China in 1882. I read it and found the terms of the contract tough and unfair towards the employee, in this case my dear grandfather who I never met. From what I heard Paolo worked hard and diligently. He was well respected and in demand. He happily settled down in Shanghai and enjoyed his working experience and the Chinese lifestyle. I treasure one of his pictures taken during his sojourns in Shanghai. Grandfather is sitting on an armchair dressed like a mandarin. He looks handsome, young, and in charge. I love this portrait of him which I will cherish for life, and hopefully my children will pass it on to their children.

While in Shanghai grandfather fell in love with a pretty Italian girl. It just happened that both of them were sailing back to Italy on the same steamer, where Paolo declared his love and intention to marry her. Her name was Giovanna, and she is my grandmother. Her answer was "yes, yes I will marry you Paolo," but she added, "If you had asked me in Shanghai I would have rather stayed there." Too late, they came back to their native country and were happily married.

Giovanna was a determined young lady who was a key factor in the extraordinarily successful career of my grandfather as a silk industrialist. As soon as my grandparents came back to Italy from China, they got married and set up their first silk filature, or *filanda* as it is called in Italy. Giovanna became the manager of this enterprise, though a lady in charge was quite a novelty in those days. Grandfather started to scout the countryside around Parabiago in order to hire young ladies to work in the plant. Grandmother started teaching the new employees the silk spinning techniques. It was not easy, but after a while she managed to train a group of young ladies to perform the job required.

Grandfather had to solve another problem in his business. These ladies had no better way to get to work than bicycling or walking long distances as there was no public transportation. Paolo, the practical industrialist, provided housing close to work.

This was not the only obstacle he had to surmount. Most of his employees were married, and their husbands often had no job. Grandfather was concerned about these unemployed individuals. He kept thinking about how to come up with an idea to correct this situation. Sure enough, he came up with a great idea. When he told his wife, my grandmother approved and told him to go ahead. His project consisted in establishing a shoe-making school to be offered to these unemployed men. Paolo hired a master shoe maker from the town of Vigevano to teach these men a trade. Vigevano is a small town in Lombardy not too far away from Parabiago, where the best handmade shoes were produced at the time. This master shoe maker started to teach the husbands of my grandfather's employees, and pretty soon these men mastered this profession. Consequently the social status of the citizens of Parabiago improved dramatically, and they started to prosper. The shoes made in Parabiago can be found in the best stores all over the world.

Another important contribution that my grandfather made to his town was providing electricity and water. Unfortunately both of my grandparents died before I was born. I often fantasize about both of them, to the point that I am jealous of my eldest sister Lalla who had the chance to enjoy them.

• • •

In Mother's family, Aunt Giuseppina was the first to get married, then Mother, then Aunt Germana and finally Uncle Piero, while Aunt Gabriella never married. For a while she lived in my grandparents' villa before moving to Milan. My grandparents' villa stood in the same compound where the first *filanda* was built, however when you entered the gate you could not see it because it was located in back of the house.

Before the war we used to visit Aunt Gabriella during the weekends or holy days. I vividly remember when our car reached the big iron gate of the villa's entrance; father would blow the car's horn and the door attendant would appear immediately, holding his hat close to his stomach and bowing gently to welcome us, then solemnly replacing his hat and opening the gate. It was a ritual, the same act every single time we visited.

To reach the villa, the car had to follow the driveway which turned around a small hill, on top of which a majestic oak tree dominated and hid the building, a nineteen century two-story which was covered by green ivy climbing up to the second floor. This place was magic for me. I was transported to another world, in another time, and I was enchanted.

Close to the villa through an arch stood the small chapel where Mother and Daddy were married.

Aunt Gabriella, a vivacious petite lady impeccably

dressed, greeted us in front of the house. She kissed us one by one in order of age. When it was my turn to kiss her I smelled cigarettes on her breath mixed with her favorite French Perfume, Shalimar. It was well known that she spent her nights reading books, waking up past lunch time every single day of the week. To me this was the ultimate daring life. I admired her, and yet I was intimidated by her eccentricity.

As soon as we entered the house we were on the loose. We ran up and down the narrow staircase. We went up to Aunt Gabriella's bedroom and into our favorite place, her boudoir, between the bedroom and the bathroom. I right away directed myself to Aunt Gabriella's vanity, which was full of colorful flasks all lined up, from the large sizes to the smallest ones. Boxes of cream for the visage, lipsticks, pink, violet, red, I was fascinated . . . I had never seen anything like that. I was tempted to try some of these beauty products, but I was afraid of Aunt Gabriella, so I just looked and wondered how she could possibly use all this stuff!

The luncheons at Aunt Gabriella's were long and tedious. The food was delicious but too elaborate. The antipasto was plentiful. She always found all the so-called *primizie*, for instance asparagus usually came in May but she managed to serve it in early April, never revealing her sources. She loved to surprise everybody with her specialties. While her dishes were being complimented by her guests, Aunt Gabriella's eyes would beam with pleasure, but I was surprised by how stern she was with her butler. Nothing was ever done the way she wanted.

At her luncheon we were usually the only guests. However, sometimes at the table sat an elderly second aunt of ours, Clementine. She had been living with Aunt Gabriella since she had become a widower a long time before. She had a little living quarter for herself where she spent almost all day, except when she went out for long walks or showed up for the meals or tea in the afternoon. I always saw her wearing black dresses, and around her neck she had a black velvet ribbon, her candid white hair gathered on top of her nape. Her complexion was as white as wax, her delicate features making her look like a picture on a cameo.

At Aunt Gabriella's luncheons I never heard Clementine participate in the conversation. At times she would give signs of approval or disapproval with her head. We would then make fun of her by chanting "Aunt Clementine agrees" or "Clementine doesn't agree" in unison. At this point Mother would dart us a disapproving look, making me feeling so guilty for having been so cruel to Aunt Clementine. I guess it was too late, the damage was done. Why did I not think before reacting this way?

We children got tired of listening to the grown-ups' conversations and became restless, so we would misbehave. Is that an excuse? I wonder. We were scolded all the time for not sitting properly, for not holding the flatware the way you were supposed to and for giggling too much.

At the end of the luncheon when the grown-ups would

sip their coffee—when we were finally excused to leave the table—we'd rush to the garden, free at last to do what we felt like. The garden in front of the house and around it was not huge, but it was beautifully kept, with greeneries and bushes. Among the trees a tall magnolia with its fat green leaves stood like a grand dame. In summertime when the heat was unbearable it was so great to sit under its cool shade.

When I was there I felt like I was alone in the world of this magic, secret place where its inhabitants lived in this magnificent magnolia tree. When no one was around, which was most of the time, they'd come out to sing and dance. The girls' dresses were made of the beautiful white magnolia flowers and boys were its green leaves. The long curly hair of the girls was braided with small pink flower bows, while the boys' long wavy hair fell on their shoulders. At the very end of the yard there was even a deep cave where the winter snow was stored to provide a cool place for perishable goods in the summer time.

I was woken up from my magic world when we were summoned for the trip back to the city, which was usually too soon for my taste. We tried all sort of tricks in the hope of delaying the departure. This upset Daddy, who would be longing to go back home. I wished I could spend more time in that fabulous place; leaving filled my heart with sadness, but maybe I was just tired.

In the car on the way back to the city, I would look at the lights of the other cars passing by. Slowly I would fall asleep together with my siblings. When we arrived home I was so sleepy it was hard to get up. At home a light dinner was served, and then we'd go to bed. The sadness was gone.

    I am home.

Chapter 4

The nights Mother and Daddy entertained their friends and acquaintances, the house looked and sounded completely different. Almost a week before the date of one such event, a big tornado was sweeping the house. Angiolino was in charge of cleaning windows, mirrors, and shining the floors. Silver dishes and flatware were polished and counted over and over. Often they, the grown-ups of course, made us do the job of counting. We enjoyed it at first, but we grew quickly bored of it and went to inspect what was going on in the kitchen. Here the maids were washing glasses, carafes, and china, all while chattering away. Table clothes were washed, ironed, and starched stiff. An electric atmosphere pervaded our household, and we loved it.

For days the menu was discussed and eventually chosen. Previous guest lists were checked in order to avoid duplication. Mother kept a record of every detail. We children knew we were considered a nuisance in this situation. Everybody had a task and no one had time to keep an eye on us. We enjoyed this. We sniffed around like hunting dogs. We went where the action was, and during these days there was plenty for sure.

When the evening of the dinner came everything was ready, like a miracle. Angiolino was on duty, parking the guests' cars. He looked decent in his black jacket and white starched shirt, his hair neatly combed. He seemed almost human. The maids were wearing their black uniforms with small white organdy aprons and white gloves with their hair pulled back. Everybody was busy fixing the last minute details, the flowers on the table, canapés to be warmed and served with the aperitifs. The wine bottles were counted to be sure that there were enough for the evening. There were so many details to be taken care of. Luckily Mother gave everyone a reminder list.

During the guests' arrival, we children positioned ourselves on top of the central marble staircase, where we could see the entrance without being seen. We stayed there until the last guest arrived, then we retreated to our rooms. My sister Baby and I shared the same bedroom. That night, because of the great excitement, we were talking and it was hard to fall asleep. We discussed the ladies' outfits. We always found Mother the most elegant and attractive one. Mother was always beautifully dressed, especially when she would go to la Scala for the Grand Opening of the Opera Season. One year she was ready and dressed before Daddy, who was late coming home from the office. There was a young woman, Gina, who had been my nanny when I was an infant and had since become the doorman of one of Daddy's buildings in central Milan. The evening of the opening at la Scala she went to see the people going into the theater, and when she spotted Mother and Daddy, she started clapping, much to the embarrassment of both of my parents. (Gina was very fond of me. When I was six months old she accompanied Mother on a trip with Daddy to Paris. Mother was still breast feeding me, so I went along too. We traveled by car, Angiolino the chauffeur, Gina, Daddy, Mother and myself. During our stay in Paris she would stroll me down the Champs-Élysées in the Tuileries. Mother would come, feed me, and then go back to her Paris engagements. After this trip Gina would talk about all the fabulous things she saw in Paris, making the other maids terribly jealous of her, to the point that Mother suggested she cool it.

On the night of the party, my sister and I admired our mother but laughed because one of the ladies wore a curious dress which did not fit her properly. My sister said, "She is really a silly goose to go around with a dress like that one!" She kept repeating "silly goose silly goose" until she sounded like a broken record and it seemed like she could not stop saying it over and over again. We laughed until tears flowed down our cheeks. We were wide awake and could not fall asleep.

I was disappointed when I found out that Mother didn't

invite our family physician, Dr. Enrico Segre, to her dinner party. He was a wonderful gentleman, handsome like a movie star. In a nutshell, after my father he was the person I admired the most. I thought the world of him. When someone was sick he would come to our house, and I would usually look out for him. I'd follow him up the stairs, trying to keep up with his long legs. I loved the way he climbed up our staircase two steps at a time. In a jiffy he was upstairs while I was still at the bottom. Sometimes I wanted to fake sickness to make him come to the house.

Mother always told me that Dr. Segre was very fond of me. She explained the reason as follows: One morning Mother picked me up from the crib—I was not even one month old—and noticed that my throat glands were swollen. She was terribly concerned. She got a hold of Dr. Segre right away, who rushed to our house and summoned Professor G. Castiglioni, a friend of my parents, as well as another famous doctor, to consult on what to do with this baby. Apparently Dr. Segre's diagnosis was the right one, in spite of his being the youngest physician of the three. They operated on my glands, and I was just fine.

The wallpaper of our bedroom was a pretty pink with green flowers. The bedspread was cotton with the same pattern. I would count the flowers, the first row, then the second one, until I was tired enough to fall asleep. Two wicker chairs in a pale green color stood in front of a medium-sized wicker table where we would do our homework. The room had three large windows, one of which opened up to a balcony. We were not allowed to open it; this balcony was going to become a bathroom one of these days, so we were told.

For the time being we used the bathroom on the right of our room, which belonged to the guest room. My sister and I very often used Mother and Daddy's bathroom, or as the family called it, *Le salon de bain*. This was a large rectangular room with a huge window facing the garden, all done in black and white marble and mirrored walls. The bathtub was grand; it could fit three of us kids. Of course, if you were in it, two was even better. My sister and I called it our swimming pool. We splashed each other and pretended to swim underwater, driving Ernesta crazy. We behaved in this wild way because we resented her presence—we did not think we needed her to chaperon us.

She would stand there like a watch dog, decent enough to let us have a jolly good time, but soon she would start grabbing my head to shampoo my hair. She would pull my hair so hard that I screamed in pain, and all the soap would end up in my eyes. I would start crying, my eyes burning badly, but she was still doing her job and not paying attention to my problem.

I hated her so violently that in trying to avoid her I fell into the bathtub, splashing her. She retreated, getting a bath towel and trying to dry herself off. She was furious; her eyeballs seemed to pop diabolically from their sockets. It was our turn to be scared, when just then the bathroom door opened and Mother came in. "Children what is going on?" We were more than happy not to say anything, and I let Ernesta rinse my hair. I heard Mother call the maid to come quickly to dry up the bathroom floor "before someone gets hurt." The marble floor was dangerously slippery when wet. My sister had her shampoo after me. I noticed that, because my mother was around, Ernesta was holding my sister's hair gently.

On the rarest occasion when Ernesta was not guarding us, I enjoyed looking at the reflection of my wet body in the mirror. I'd gather the shampoo suds on top my head like a wig. I'd look in the mirror and my sister would laugh, saying, "You look like a portrait of that lady hanging on the wall in the entrance hall."

My youngest brother Mario slept upstairs in the nursery. The staff lodged up there as well. Close to the servant quarters there was a huge storage room. It was wood-paneled, and the shelves were full to capacity with packages of spaghetti, burlap bags filled with rice, flour, sugar, walnut, pecans, and chocolate bars. This room was usually locked up, but sometimes when the supplies were being delivered the door would be open and we'd sneak in, aiming sometimes for the burlap bag containing the dry raisins. We'd make a little hole in the burlap bag, not too big, otherwise the raisins would run all over the floor. We'd fish out the raisins and fill a paper bag we'd carried up for this purpose.

But the chocolate was our favorite target. Father bought these chocolate bars when he went to Lugano, Switzerland. It was the very bitter kind, squeezing you inside with an amazing bittersweet taste while in your mouth. Sometimes it could make you shiver, it was so delicious. When one got close to the chocolate bar it was completely another matter. First of all, the eagerness to get a piece of that juicy chocolate was so strong that one would panic and try to get a piece with your own bare hands. Forget it; it was so hard that no human hand, even a very strong one, could break even a little tiny piece. Time was limited, what could one do? I was convinced we'd need a hammer and scalpel to be able to get a piece of that wonderful aromatic temptation. So for the time being we'd give up and wait until they served us a piece.

Chapter 5

In Milan, when Daddy was in town he'd drive us to school in the mornings. Those days were my favorite ones. It was so great to talk to him, to see his lovely head sitting in front of me in the car. He filled my heart with joy. His hair was blondish brown, the shape of his head so proportioned . . . he was so handsome I could not keep my eyes off him. It was especially wonderful to hear his voice; he would often come home so late at night that we did not have the chance to see him.

I would get scared at night, mostly when I was in bed in the dark. I'd hear all those strange, scary night sounds: a dog barking, the credulous sound of the tram passing by in front of our house, the raucous voice of a drunk, the cracking sound of the parquets, or the wind hitting shutters. I'd desperately close my eyes and sink my head into the cold pillow. Once, deep into the night, the entrance doorbell rang. I heard fearful sounds, and my heart stopped beating for a split second. I heard the sound of hurried steps . . . then the night fell silent again. My sister was sleeping; I heard her breathing quietly, a reassuring sound. After a while I fell asleep as well.

At breakfast the topic of conversation was the mysterious ringing bell during the night. Everyone had an explanation. "A cat, maybe." "Come on, it's not possible." Then everybody was laughing. The prevailing explanation was that the night disturbance was perpetrated by a drunken man. We were all satisfied with the answer, and we carried on with our everyday lives. I pretended to be thirsty and asked for a glass of water. In the kitchen I heard different comments on the subject. Apparently the night visitors were Luchino Visconti and his partner in mischief, the heir to the Italian throne, Prince Umberto di Savoia. I was speechless. These ladies must have been joking... I could not believe what I was hearing! Luchino Visconti's mother was a friend of my father's, and I knew how worried she was about her son. He was a well-known scoundrel. Luchino Visconti belonged to a noble Milanese family dating back to 1395 when Milan became a Ducat under the Visconti. Since those times things had changed. Even in our time the Visconti family was considered respectable nobility. With good lineage but not much power or wealth left, Luchino's father married money. He married the daughter of the owner of the pharmaceutical Empire Carlo Erba, my father's friend. I heard that Luchino was very successful with his thoroughbred horses; he kept them at the stable near his *garconniere* in San Siro, not even a mile from our house.

I ran upstairs breathless, looking for Mother. I was dying to tell her what I had heard in the kitchen. How shocking, and maybe a little amusing . . . I found myself smiling. However I could not believe grown-ups were behaving so childishly. On my way up I met Ernesta and asked her if she knew where Mother was. She told me she was out shopping. I stopped for a while, leaning against the banister of the staircase, then slowly I descended. But I would not forget this event.

I knew that Luchino was a well-known playboy and the subject of town gossip. In the kitchen I had learned that he kept a *garconniere*. I did not know exactly what this French word meant. It sounded interesting, *garconniere, garconniere,* I liked to say it over and over again. I was not the gossiping type, but I was curious and loved to be up to date with events. When eventually I got to ask Mother about the night call and the gossip I heard in the kitchen she dismissed it by saying it was just a joke, silly maybe, but just a joke.

I, however, was determined to pursue this matter further by first looking up the word *garconniere* in the French dictionary, which I knew was somewhere in the bookshelves in the library. I looked and looked, and after a while I saw it up on the very top shelf out of my reach. I desperately needed help. Where should I go for it? Of course to the kitchen, where else? It was the wrong time of day, though I wondered when the right time would have been. Everybody was busy preparing dinner and no one paid any attention to my request. Disgusted, I stole food from the serving platter and was chased out of the kitchen.

Luckily, on my way back to the library I met my sister Lalla, and she kindly agreed to give me a hand. I didn't tell her why I needed the French dictionary; she didn't ask, so I didn't have to come up with an excuse. Good, I was happy and carried my precious dictionary to my room. In the silence of my room–my sister was probably playing somewhere else, thank God–I consulted the dictionary. I was excited and not familiar with all those pages of French words, so it took me some time to spell *garconniere* correctly. "A bachelor pad where boys take their girlfriends." Now I understood why the girls in the kitchen were endlessly giggling. I was surprised and felt a little ashamed and guilty. Why, I do not know, but I did. I closed the dictionary as fast as I could and ran down to return it to its place, but of course I could not reach the upper shelf, so I left it on the table.

I was a little confused but I kept my secret to myself. I tried not to think about or elaborate on what I found out about Luchino's chalet close to his stables. However, it wasn't easy to forget something so exciting, intriguing and new to me. What do those guys actually do when they're all together? I asked myself. I didn't have an answer, so my imagination started flying. A guilty feeling crept in, so I tried to distract myself. But it wasn't easy.

Chapter 6

We children and our mother spend the first month of war at Lake Maggiore. We take long walks and bicycle rides, and the ferryboat touring the lake's little villages. There are not too many visitors, just the villagers, and the streets are empty, like ghost towns. Mother says it is kind of special, but we do not agree. We like crowded places.

So far the war hasn't affected us, and then the radio daily news announces that Mussolini's troops are moving toward the French border.

But I am happy because I meet my first admirer, a young boy, whose name is Livio Sichirollo. Mother is a friend of his parents, so we are often invited for tea and games at their home. They have a nineteenth century villa surrounded by a park of secular trees. We enjoy playing in the woods; it is cool and beautiful, the smell of trees is so strong I breathe it in, and it fills my lungs. I feel great.

Livio usually greets us all dressed up like a pirate, one

black patch covering his right eye and a wooden sword hanging from his belt. He is a couple of years older than me, and it is very special to have an older admirer. He cannot keep his eyes off me, and that makes my sisters giggle most of the time, also giving them a good reason to tease me.

One morning Mother tells us that it has been decided to leave the lake and go to the shore. We are going to Finalmarina, a small town north of Genoa. We are all very happy and look forward to going to the seashore. The lake is beautiful, but swimming in the blue Mediterranean Sea is much more alluring.

Finalmarina is a combination of three villages: Finalborgo is situated inland, while Finalmarina and Finalpia are along the Mediterranean shore. Our family owns a tiny apartment in Finalpia on the shore. This apartment is so tiny compared to our house in Milan that Mother, referring to its dimension, calls it "the doll house" (nothing to do with Ibsen's play).

If one arrives from Genoa like we do, coming from Milan by car, we use the Via Aurelia. Approaching the village of Finalpia you go through a tunnel on top of which an old Saracen tower stands surrounded by contorted, centuries-old olive trees. This spot is known as the lamed goat, or Capra Zoppa. This tower has been used in the past as an observatory to spot the enemy galleons coming from the sea. The view is breathtaking, and often the wind is strong. It is cool in the summer time, which makes it a good place to go to. When we were young, Mother would pack our lunches, with the help of Ernesta, for a *déjeuner sur l'herbe* under the ancient olive trees.

Finalpia is close to a colorful fishing village called Finalmarina, which is reachable through a littoral of tall palm trees, a colorful, ornate promenade of beautifully kept gardens and flowers. During the hot summer days, the tall shade of the palms and the cool fresh breeze coming in from the Mediterranean makes this promenade a pleasure. Full moon nights especially are carved in my memory, like a still life painted by a naïf artist, the moon so big, so round, so red!

The Finalese history, like that of so many places in Italy, can be traced back to the Byzantine and Longobardi time. There are vestiges of the Roman Empire scattered all over the territory: ruins like bridges, walls, and arches. Romans were interested mostly in the coastlines—the inland was not of much interest to them, being difficult to conquer and too poor to manage. Upon the fall of the Roman Empire, in the ninth and tenth centuries, the Saracen started to invade the Liguria Coast lines. In the year 1186 the Marchese Del Carretto established his residency in the Finalese and became the absolute ruler in this strategically located territory. It was not an easy job for him to keep his supremacy in the region; the Genoa Republic was always threatening his domain. The Spanish, the French, and other neighboring powers constantly threatened to invade. The Finalese community has never been a prosperous one. Its inhabitants were mainly fishermen. The Finalese location, however, is a strategic one with easy access to Lombardy and Piedmont for the trading of goods. All of this explains why over the centuries many have aspired to conquer this territory.

Halfway from Finalpia to Finalmarina, overlooking the littoral on top of a rocky hill, stands a castle called Castle Franco. During the war it is a charming ruin called Shanghai. In this fortress lives a poor community who made its home here having no other place to live. Many children and cats run loose day and night. A beautiful young lady called the Queen of Shanghai lives there and rules the place. It is believed that most of those children running loose are her sons and daughters.

I remember the day when we went up to visit the Castel Franco. For us children from a sophisticated city like Milan, we find Castel Franco utterly fascinating. For us, this fortress is full of mystery, its inhabitants so different from the people we know. The fortress itself with those ancient thick high walls, towers, turrets, and labyrinth passages make our imaginations fly.

Many times we kids have tried to explore the fortress. One morning we decide it is the right time to go up and conquer it. To reach the entrance, which is at the very top, one has to climb up a steep stone stairway. The entrance branches off in various narrow passages. The first on the right is an observatory tower so narrow that two slim people can barely stand inside it. The strong July sun is hitting our bare heads. The pungent smell of urine, coming from the observatory tower next to us, is unbearable. We wisely move quickly away from this place. We pause for a while, catching our breath. I am perspiring so much that my light cotton shirt is wet and sticks to my body.

Everything is still around us. A couple of cats cross our path mewing desperately. I feel uneasy and weary, as if someone is watching us. I look around, but I see no one.

We sit on a stone wall. The stones are hot, my rear end is burning, and I am uncomfortable with no escape from the strong hot sun in sight. Suddenly a group of half-naked kids storms around us. There is no aggression in their bodies, they just stare at us as if we are some kind of different species. One of these boys is smiling at me. Eventually this young guy became my ball boy at the tennis club.

I have barely said hello and the boys disappear as quickly as they came. We look at each other and start descending the long stairway, happy to go back home.

• • •

Finally, all packed, we take off by train for the Mediterranean shore. We children are restless and happy at the idea of the train ride: Mother, my two brothers, Domenico and Mario Jr., my sister Gabriella, Ernesta the governess, and myself. Lalla, the eldest sister, is going to

Milan to join Father to resume her art education at the Brera Academy. The thought that we will soon be able to swim in the blue Mediterranean Sea puts me in a joyous mood. I cannot keep still for a second, upsetting everyone with my restless mood. Ernesta keeps pulling my hair in order to stop my jumping around.

The train voyage is a welcome adventure. I love to sit in the compartment with other people, look at them and study the way they look and behave. Never mind if the train ride is long. I look out of the window and see green fields, the trees, and houses passing by me like in a moviola, but the rhythm of the images is faster.

I like when the train stops at the various stations. As soon as the train stops, the food vendors on the station platform offer their merchandise, screaming "*Panini imbottiti, focaccia, aranciate San Pellegrino!*" They scream at the top of their lungs in order to be heard by the passengers, holding their food trays above their heads. Making their way through a myriad of passengers carrying luggage, dragging along children of all ages, I admire how these vendors manage to keep all the food in place.

My head is spinning as some of our fellow passengers get hold of their belongings and rush out of the compartment. Evidently their trip is over; they've reached their destination. Immediately someone else peeps in and, seeing the vacant seats, comes in and sits comfortably with a sign of relief in his face. This change of the guard keeps our interest alive.

What really gets my sister Baby's and my attention is a group of handsome young navy officers. The train stops at Genoa station, and this city has one of the main northern Italian naval harbors. These young officers are wearing their elegant blue uniforms, so the two of us are literally hanging out of the train window, pushing each other, competing for the best view. I feel the strong hand of Ernesta holding me back, and without a single word she pulls up the train window. In the same instant the train leaves, slowly at first, then gradually gaining speed with a crescendo whistling sound. I am very disappointed to leave this colorful station. I hear Mother talking to a gentleman sitting close to her. He says that the Italian naval fleet is in Genoa ready to set sea to fight the enemy. Our euphoria is tempered by this comment.

I'd forgotten about being at war. We are silent now, and I doze away to the lullaby of the train's movement.

After a couple of stops our destination, the Finalmarina station, comes up. I wake up from my torpor when our train stops with a screeching, breaking sound. We collect our belongings and troop down the train steps. The balmy sea breeze hits us with its strong salty smell. Our arrival is triumphant. We are the only passengers getting out of the train. Old Baccicin, the porter with his big belly sticking out from his shirt, greets us. With no taxicabs in front of the station, we take a horse-drawn carriage to go home to Finalpia.

A ride in a horse-drawn cab is my favorite kind. The horse

pulling this cab is not a fine example of its species. It is a big powerful animal, but its main focus is swishing its tail around gently trying to get rid of the sticky afternoon flies. The sound of the horse shoes on the asphalt is like a happy song. The wind is caressing my hair, my face, my entire body—it feels so good. I breathe the salty air; it is exhilarating. People in the street wave to us. We laugh and wave back.

What a luminous day. The sun is still bright even if it is late afternoon. The blue Mediterranean Sea is calm. We go through the almost deserted streets, and the sound of the horse's steps echoes around us.

When we arrive, the house is spick and span, the windows are wide open, and the sky is getting pink with the approaching sunset. A strong jasmine smell permeates the air. I look at the sea in front of my window, and I see it is turning pink. My heart is full of joy.

We eat a light supper, and we are ready to go to bed. Ernesta doesn't have to scold us to turn the light off; we are dead tired. I fall asleep as soon as I put my head on the soft, humid pillow. Every window in the house is properly sealed off with heavy, dark curtains so that no light will show outside. You get in trouble with the police if this happens. They say the enemy can spot the light and drop bombs.

The apartment is located close to the beach, near a pier. This morning we heard from the milk man that the military is going to install at the very tip of the jetty a photoelectric device in order to detect enemy planes and ships. All of a sudden the calm, blue Mediterranean Sea does not look so peaceful anymore. Even so I do not see anything on the horizon.

In the morning, our first one, we are up early for a quick breakfast then off to the beach, which is just in front of our house. The beach is deserted, no sun umbrellas, no chaise lounges with people sunning themselves, no children playing or swimming in the sea. The beach is deserted and seems huge to my eyes.

The only activity we see is men in military uniforms working at the pier. We are tempted to go closer to see what they are doing, but we choose not to, and when we tell Mother she compliments us for being so wise. At lunch everybody is commenting on the installation of the photoelectric device. Is the enemy going to bomb us? We have not forgotten the air raid in Milan on the first day of war, which was not even a month ago. Why would the enemy bombs us? We are not a strategic military spot! Are we? Mother says not to worry.

After a couple of days we get used to the machine, as we call it. We do not discuss it anymore. It is accepted. Our life goes on pleasantly, we swim, we eat, we play and suddenly one morning we wake up and it is September. Mother enrolls us at the Elementary School in Finalpia.

The war, I guess, is going on. If you listen to the radio the war bulletins say that Mussolini is conquering the world together with the Germans, France is in our hands, etc. etc.

We go to school and make friends with the local children. I enjoy the weather, the surrounding hills, the inland with those beautiful silver-green olive trees. Close to our house there is a 1930s style hotel called GB for its owner's initials. He has two sons, Benito and Angelo, called Pillin. We become good friends. Benito, the oldest, had a crush on me since we met. He wants to be my partner in every game we play. I am flattered; his attitude reminds me very much of Livio. The two-story hotel is long, narrow, and shaped like a model of a wooden ship. There are no guests at the hotel right now. We often play here, and it is great to be able to run through the narrow empty corridors playing hide and seek. I am surprised to hear the echoes of our steps and voices following us around. I've never in my life, so far, had so much fun.

At night I am so exhausted that I fall asleep as soon as my head touches the pillow. In the city our life was so different. Here in Finale we are free to talk to everybody. We can walk where we like, as long as we tell Ernesta our whereabouts. It is so extraordinary! I enjoy this freedom to the full extent.

1940 came dramatically but passed by smoothly, for us.

The public school I attend here in this small village of the Italian Riviera is very different from the one I attended in Milan. I am referring to the teaching, the school supplies, the assistance given to each student. It's black and white. You learn your lesson by the textbooks with little explanation given; you have to learn the way it is written. In Milan it was a girl's school, while here in Finalpia it's for boys and girls.

My teacher is a nun named Anna Maria. She is a petite woman with a short temper. While teaching she carries a long, narrow bamboo stick that she uses to hit the head of any student who doesn't pay attention or talks or sleeps. Sometimes if you do something bad, she makes you put both hands on top of the desk, and from her dais she hits you with her long bamboo stick. All of this is completely new to me.

Classes are easier than in the city. Generally speaking, the boys are not very good students. Many live up in the hills and work in the fields to help their families; consequently they have a long walk in the morning to reach the school. Often they are late for classes, forget their homework or books, and have not studied.

Sister Anna Maria gets upset easily. I do understand her frustration. She cannot see any improvement in these boys' performance. Sometimes she even screams to get through those hard heads, calling them "*zucche pateche*," watermelon heads. "Translation, empty heads!" she screams out of frustration. But it doesn't help. The boys get more confused. I feel sorry for them, and I try not to look, and I keep my head down pretending to read my book. The girls are better students than the boys. They pay attention to the teacher and try hard to please her by following the lesson diligently. Girls come to class on time with their hair neatly combed, properly dressed in the white school uniform.

One day in early spring I found in my desk a bouquet of daisies with no card. I pretend not to be surprised. I just look around to see the reactions of the boys. Sure enough, one of them, as soon as I meet his eye, ducks behind the top of his desk. When he emerges I smile and his face gets all red and he looks away. After that day I frequently find in my desk when I come into class, depending on the season, one juicy peach, or an orange, or sometimes a little flower. I do not show it, but deep down it feels good and makes me smile. My admirer is Salvatore, and the poor fellow is teased by the whole class.

Classes are boring, time goes by slowly, but my sister and I have a wonderful time. We are free to go where we please. Once in a while Ernesta checks on us, but she is not like she used to be in the city. She gives us space. We take it gladly.

Students carry to school a *cartella*, or carry-on, usually made of vinyl. Besides the text and exercise books, each one carries a pen and pencil holder. This pen or pencil holder is usually made of fabric and filled with pencils, crayons, and pens called *cannuccie*, and a little box containing various sizes of nibs which are inserted into the top of the *cannuccia*. In order to be able to write you have to dip the nib into the ink pot, which is on the top of the school desk. Homework and all kinds of assignments have to be written in ink because the use of pencils is not allowed. Pencils are used for drawing only. Paper is scarce and expensive. Pencils and blotting paper are difficult to find. Blotting paper is needed to dry the ink when you are finished with your writing and carefully blot the written page. This has to be done gently and firmly to prevent the page from shifting, which could cause the smearing of the page. Surely I do not want this to happen. I learn to be careful and pay attention to what I am doing. If you are not careful while doing homework, it might happen that you smear the page and ruin it beyond repair. I tell you what; you think you can fix the smear by using an eraser? Forget it. Ink is not a pencil. The first time I erased a smear on the page of my homework I made a hole. I cried my heart out.

I learned my lesson, however. God forbid a drop of liquid falls on your ink-written homework and you have the same problem, or even worse. I manage to master it and am careful to do what is required.

We go to school, come back, play, eat, and go to bed happily. We learn that our sister Lalla is going with a friend to Venice to the Lido. How chic—I am impressed indeed. She is there with the wife of a close friend of our father and we know she likes glamour. I am awfully jealous. I wish I could be there with her. I've heard so much about Venice—the beautiful palaces, the churches, the gondolas on the Canal Grande . . . how terribly romantic! Lalla is so lucky. I wish I could be there with her.

Lalla sends us photos taken at the Lido, and in one of them she is wearing a two-piece bathing suit. She looks like a Hollywood movie star. Indeed we all agree that she looks happy and fabulous. I examine carefully every single snapshot that Lalla sends us. I picture myself sitting in a gondola, slowly navigating along the Canal Grande, admiring the beautiful architecture of the palaces and churches, feeling so good.

A loud voice wakes me up from my day dream. "Gioietta, is time to go to school."

Chapter 7

The war, so far, is far away for us, physically as well as mentally. However, things may be gradually changing. It is the beginning of 1941, just one year since the declaration of war, and food, especially meat, is hard to get. So is sugar and salt. At night we are more frequently awoken by the sound of the air raid sirens. It is quite scary to wake up to the sound of the siren, but we are getting used to it. It is no longer a shock. It is something that happens, and we do not complain anymore. We dress and run to the shelter as fast as possible. We are slowly getting used to the curfew, the food scarcity, the air raids, the lack of books, records . . . all the things that one takes for granted. I miss my daddy, my house, my school friends and relatives.

Life goes on, and thank God we are healthy. Actually we have never been so well—no colds, fevers or any other diseases. We know the local doctor, who lives with his family across the street from us. One evening we have to cross the street to summon Dr. Fasce. While eating fish, Mother gets a bone stuck in her throat. We are all concerned and a little panicky. We do not know what to do to help her out of her misery. Mother looks visibly uncomfortable. Mother gestures for us to be calm. "We should call Dr. Fasce right away," I say with a peremptory tone. Ernesta asks, "Should I go?" It is seven p.m. and curfew is just starting. Dr. Fasce is just across the street. "Go," we all tell her, "fast."

After a matter of ten minutes, which to me seems an eternity, the doctor is knocking at our door, and we are all happy to see him. In a jiffy he liberates mother from the fish bone. Mother thanks Dr. Fasce for his performance and offers him a drink. It is his turn to thank Mother, and he does so by bending his head while taking Mother's hand from the dinner table and kissing it gently. We are all eyes and ears.

Now Dr. Fasce is sitting comfortably at the dinner table with all of us. Ernesta is serving a beautiful basket of fresh fruits, serving him first of course, being the guest. But he looks at her and says, "Madam first, please." At this point I am amused and look at him more closely. After complimenting Mother for the good quality of the fruit, politely he enquires where she has bought it. Mother answers, "I get my vegetable and fruits from your neighbor, Sestimio."

"I have suspected that, for me he has the best produce in all the region, indeed."

We are lucky to have him, we all agree.

After this exchange about the good quality of Sestimio's

produce, and his honesty, Dr. Fasce goes on to tell a lot of gossip which is circulating around town. I personally get bored, so I do not get any enjoyment out of Fasce's stories. Even Mother seems to be smiling less. Maybe she is trying to give him a message, which of course he doesn't get and keeps talking. Little by little—I should say one by one—we excuse ourselves and leave the dining room, leaving Mother alone with her guest.

My sister and I are in agreement that Dr. Fasce is a pompous, boring person. We both find his son, whose name is Nini, far more amusing and entertaining. Often we meet him on our way to school and stop to chat with him. His sense of humor is most enjoyable.

The war so far for us children is far away, and it is hard to understand what it is really all about. We do not feel the impact of being at war yet. However, we see changes in our everyday life, and certainly they are not for the better. It is difficult to make a list of changes because there are many. Our lives are always the same: we wake up in the morning, we have breakfast, go to school, return, have lunch, do our homework, play, have dinner, and go to bed for a good night's sleep. It does sound boring and yet I like it; I like the regularity of the days. I enjoy the walk from school to the house. It very seldom gets cold. Sometimes the wind gets kind of forceful and you have to bundle up, and I like when this happens. The sky is beautifully clear, the wind is whistling between our ears. My sister Baby and I run with the wind. It is a great sensation; literally the wind pushes us. Other times instead there is no wind, and everything is peaceful and still. The sea is calm, shining under the sunlight. These days are my favorite ones, and I always hope they last longer.

In Milan it was not possible to enjoy the freshness of the outdoor life. We were lucky to have a big garden where we could play and have fun. But here, what a difference! I like when the sun is not strong but soft and gentle. I feel I am part of nature, like a tree or dare I say a flower, basking in the sun from morning until night.

The only things I miss are Daddy, my school, my friends, and my house.

It is the beginning of 1941, exactly one year since the declaration of war. To me it seems much longer than one year. It seems long ago when we were happily together as a big family. Was that a dream? Was it? Food like noodles, rice, sugar, and butter we often can't find. The store keeper would say, "Come back tomorrow, maybe we will get some." To say nothing of meat, which has disappeared from the meat stores, where if you are lucky you can get poultry which is locally produced.

At night we are more frequently awakened by the sound of the air raid sirens, which sound like screaming voices. We have to get up from our friendly beds, get dressed more or less, and run to the shelter. The shelter is almost a mile away, and to reach it we have to walk, or better yet run, through the via Aurelia, which could be one target of the enemy planes. When the moon is full the shade of the huge airplanes follows us. It is hard to describe how I feel. It is so scary. I feel my legs getting weak, and I am trying to keep up with the others. The way to the shelter is so long. Are they going to kill us? Why? Why should they want to target us? We are not a military outpost, are we? I wonder why nations have to be at war; this is beyond my comprehension. Probably I do not understand all the various interests and businesses involved.

I am running fast trying to keep up with the grown-ups. I feel my heart in my mouth, and I want to spit it out. What an awful feeling. The enemy airplanes are on top of us; their shadows obscure the moon. It seems they want to suck us up like giant monsters. The roar of the airplane engines is loud but low. I hear screams. Someone is saying, "Stop running, take shelter, stop, stop." I do not know what to do, so I stay as close as possible to Mother and the others. We stop near a small wall along the road, piling up one on top of the other. It seems time has stopped for good. Suddenly the heavy roar of the airplanes is no more. The night is silent again. We hear the voices of the grown-ups urging us to move as fast as possible in order to get to the shelter before the second wave of enemy bombers reaches us.

Finally, exhausted, we reach the tunnel. Many people

already crowd the air shelter. In the darkness they seem like ghosts or inhabitants of Dante's inferno. I am frightened and stay close to Mother and my sisters and brothers. Mother consoles us by saying it will be over before we know it. "You will see," she says.

The sound of the cease alarm siren reaches us an hour or so later. We go back home. When I am out of the tunnel I am relieved to see that everything is exactly as it was when we came in. I am so tired I barely reach my bed and fall asleep immediately.

After school when the days are mild, we take long walks. Ernesta leads us along a narrow path up the hills where the secular olive trees dominate the valley with their majestic dark trunks and vaporous silver gray leaves. In the month of February we find the first violets that grow close to the stone walls. We make beautiful bouquets to bring home to Mother. From up here the Mediterranean looks blue and immense. How peaceful it is when we are all alone.

At night, however, the enemy air raids are getting more frequent. The war bulletins are somber, even the voice of the announcer is subdued. It seems that in Africa our troops have armament and supply problems. That is so bad for the morale of our poor soldiers. The grown-ups are concerned and disturbed by the actual situation of the war. Everyday life is changing.

It's clear we Italians chose the wrong ally. The

Rome/Berlin/Tokyo Axis is a disaster of gigantic proportions. It is also called the "Iron Pact." I guess the iron is rusting quickly. It's still 1941.

Father now rarely comes to visit us. The trip from Milan to Finalpia is both difficult and dangerous. The railways are daily targets. Our allies, the Germans, use the trains to transport heavy war equipment like artillery, tanks, cannons, military vehicles, and troops. The English bombers, the RAF, keep shelling the main arteries of our little country. The Mail Service is often late and frequently the letters we receive have been opened. The Fascist regime has the power to open any letters in the mail and erase whatever they think is against the party. Consequently often we get letters full of ugly black lines erasing the words.

The letters we get from Daddy are short, and the only subjects are his health and Lalla's progress in her art classes. Any other subject is avoided. We are glad to receive them anyway.

Aliments are rationed but little is available in the stores anyhow. Ration cards are often useless. One night after dinner the doorbell rings. We children are not supposed to answer the door, especially at night. We look at each other, it being very unusual to hear the doorbell, and it is a little frightening. After a while the maid comes in and whispers something to Mother. Our eyes are focused on mother; we see her getting up from her seat and leaving the room without uttering a word. We are somewhat shocked. We know that there is a curfew and no one who has some common sense ventures out into the streets. May be it is not yet nine p.m., which is the time when the curfew is enforced.

After a while Mother comes back, and almost in unison we ask her, "Who was he? What did he or she want? Do you know this person?" Mother doesn't answer but sits and starts checking our papers.

We are terribly disappointed.

The next day, we find out that the phantom night visitor was a man offering meat and other commodities on the black market. We are not supposed to know this, and we are forbidden to talk to anyone about it. We learn how this transaction works. The first contact takes the order and sets the price of the merchandise, and after the goods have been delivered to the customer, he collects the money. The location of the delivery is never the same. It is strictly forbidden and punishable by law to buy on the black market. We know that and keep quiet. Food is hard to find, but we are lucky, though, because behind our house, just across the Via Aurelia, there is an orchard, and its owner, whose name is Sestimo (he probably got his name because he was the sixth child in his family) sells us his wonderful, fresh produce.

Salt is another vital commodity which is not available anymore. One morning I am listening to Mother talking to Ernesta, who is complaining about reaching the end of the house salt supply. She is explaining to Mother that when she went that morning to buy salt at the tobacconist, he told her that not only does he not have salt anymore, but that the government will not make any further deliveries. The government, besides salt, also has a monopoly over tobacco products, cigarettes, and cigars. "What are we going to do?" asks Ernesta.

I see Mother taking her time before giving an answer. Then she says, "Why don't we make salt ourselves? We have this beautiful Mediterranean Sea in front of us, why not use its water?"

I am astonished. I am thinking that Mother is a genius. I feel like jumping, so I start jumping up and down in the room. "Stop jumping, Gioietta, please," Mother says.

A couple of days later, we come back from school and right away I notice that in front of the house, against a wall that is exposed to sunlight all day long, there is an amazing installation: corrugated metal sheets of zinc have been placed against the wall, positioned in a way to allow the salted water to stand still in their grooves. Furthermore, I notice that in the grooves crystal specks of white stuff are surfacing. I come closer and put my finger into the groove. I turn around to look at my sister and in unison we scream, "It is salt!"

Our scream is so loud that after a second the whole household is looking out of the windows. I keep looking at the narrow grooves where these white crystalline particles shine in the sun, some of them making beautiful designs. It is fascinating, and I am very much taken by it. In the afternoon my friend Renata Regis comes to visit me, and she too is deeply impressed by Mother's project. I am thinking that maybe we can go into business and sell our salt production! That would be such a great opportunity for us. I tell my sister my great idea, and she looks at me and says, "Well I guess we'll need a bigger space, don't you think?" I fully agree with her. For a while we talk about the project and how to deal with it.

At dinner these days the topic of conversation is, of course, the salt project. My sister and I look at each other and I proceed to tell Mother our interest in getting into the salt business—to produce salt and sell it. Mother smiles and says, "Well that is not a bad project, however you have to consider the great work it will be to prepare, and not only that but the large quantity of sea water you'll need in order to produce a large quantity of salt to sell." We quietly listen to her, and we understand that it is too ambitious of a project.

But I say, "Salt is so vital to the health of human beings, as you always tell us. It is important to do something like this."

"I agree," Mother says, "but I think one has to be qualified in order to do a good job, right?" Reluctantly, I agree with her reasoning.

The conversation about salt, however, is not over yet. Someone asks why the government handles the production and distribution of salt. "I assume," says Mother, "that first of all the handling of sea water belongs to the country.

Therefore it's government business, and the government can afford the cost of production. Clear?" Mother adds, "You know that in Tuscany, and I believe in Umbria too, the bread is unsalted?"

We look at each other, puzzled. "Why?"

"Well, in the seventeenth century, during the Papal Sovereignty, the Vatican charged a tax on salt, so the inhabitants of the region refused to pay this tax and made their daily bread without it. The bread there is still unsalted." The word "disgusting" echoed. Can you believe bread without salt? Disgusting is the word! Fruit is being served, so we calm down and concentrate on choosing our fruit.

One day while coming back from school we notice a big commotion of people coming in and out of the main door. Right away we try to find out what it's all about. We learn that a lady with two daughters is moving into the apartment above one of the ladies who takes care of the premises, whose name is Pina. Pina is quite a character, very well known in the village for being colorful. In her vernacular I personally find her extremely amusing, as does my sister. But Ernesta doesn't like her at all and keeps complaining to Mother about Pina's work ethic. "She talks too much and doesn't work enough." But I find her amusing and enjoy interpreting her strong Genovese accent. I love to listen to comments about people we know.

I decide to look for Pina in order to get some first-hand information about the new arrival. I have been looking for her everywhere, but there's no sight of her. She is always running around doing errands for everybody, and like Ernesta she talks, talks, talks. I give up my search for Pina and stop at the tobacconist to chat with the owner, who is my friend, because every day I buy the *Corriere della Sera* for mother. I have been there for a while when Pina comes into the store, and without my even asking her, she proceeds to tell us about this lady from Genoa who just arrived with her twin daughters, who she calls "my little girls." "I tell you those girls are ready to get married." Pina pauses for a second, looks around to be sure everyone present heard what she said, then starts laughing her head off. Then she adds, "She is one of those ladies who refuses to get old. She is beautiful, mind you." We start laughing too, and she seems to be satisfied that her audience is having a good time. She turns around and leaves the store without a word.

I run home to tell Mother what we've learned about the new tenant. Mother listens patiently, but we are upset by her remarks. "Please girls, do not pay any attention to what Pina says. She is making things up to please her audience; it is her way of having fun."

Two weeks after, a Genovese gentleman arrives. I hear Pina coming in. She is singing some kind of a song, and I cannot make out the words. Then she comes closer to me, and I hear her singing a popular tune with her own words, "smell of lovers." She is repeating it over and over again in a loud voice. She wants to be sure that everybody hears her message. God, what is she up to now? "I am sure she has had one too many this morning, that's what I think, if you ask me," I tell my sister, who starts giggling.

I direct myself immediately towards the kitchen; where else should I go to get the scoop? Sure enough, the topic of discussion is indeed "The Lover," in capital letters. Nothing so glamorous has ever happened around here. The kitchen help is so busy gossiping they do not even notice our presence. Everybody has something to add. "Do you know that this guy is a medium?"

"What do you mean?" someone asks.

"Well, he has supernatural powers, that's why he is also called 'the santone.'" I feel the tension among those present with that last sentence. I am upset with myself for not having yet had the chance to see him. Does anyone know when this gentleman shows up?

Suddenly the kitchen door opens, and Mother comes in. We leave in a hurry.

One day after I have mostly forgotten the gentleman, he is right in front of me while I am coming out of the main door and he is stepping in. He stops, gently bends his head in a respectable greeting, smiles and says, "Good day to you young lady." I am confused, and I know I am blushing. I feel my cheeks burning. It is my turn to bend my head, in embarrassment, and by the time I look up he is gone. Once again I am unhappy. I had the chance to talk to him, or at least look at him, and I blew it! Shoot.

I tell my sister Baby about my brief encounter and my failure to engage him in dialogue of any sort, but I mention to her that I had the time to see his dark-haired head and his long, dark beard. It is so long it reaches the white collar of his shirt. "Really?" she asks.

"Yes, believe me. I wish you were there with me. Maybe he has magic power—I actually blushed and you know I never do that." We both start laughing.

At dinner we tell Mother all the gossip going around town, about the beautiful lady and her lover Santone. Mother seems amused. I am encouraged, and I say everybody agrees that he is a Santone, but Mother isn't excited. "I met him, you know, and I felt his power first hand." A loud burst of laughter breaks in like an explosion.

Like everything, we get used to the Santone, the beautiful temptress, and the twin sisters. We go on with our everyday lives. More gossip and new details emerge once in a while, but even Pina doesn't sing her tune anymore. Too bad; it was a lot of fun. The novelty is always interesting at first, but then it gets stale and we go looking for something new to stimulate our imaginations, which need to be stimulated all the time. I guess this takes care of our beloved Santone. Either we got used to the idea of having him around, or we simply do not care anymore.

Behind our house there is an orchard where oranges, lemons, peaches, and apricots grow. Sestimio is the owner.

Sestimio has a field where he cultivates all sorts of vegetables, artichokes, string beans, zucchini, and wonderful, juicy red tomatoes. Every two days or so, Sestimio shows up at the house with a large basket full of produce. In the winter he brings us the most incredibly large oranges called Pernambuco, so deliciously juicy. He also grows the largest tangerines I have ever seen or tasted. In the summer his juicy peaches and apricots are sensational. Sestimio is a strong, tall man. His hands are huge, and his sun-tanned face is marked with deep lines, his hair a blondish grey. For being such a big man he is quite gentle and soft-spoken. He doesn't talk much, but he is always courteous and keeps us informed about his best produce of the season. Sometimes he complains gently about the situation without really mentioning what he is referring to. It is difficult for him to sell produce to his customers out of town. There is no means of transportation.

I love to go to Sestimio's orchard when the peaches and apricots are ripe. The stillness of the field under the bright sun, and the strong, sweet smell of the ripe peaches and apricots penetrates my senses. It is a satisfying feeling.

Mother has a lady friend, a widower who took up knitting and became so good she started a profitable business. Her name is Teresita, and she is plump, pleasant, unpretentious and fun to be with. I like her a lot; she treats us children like people and entertains us with stories of her youth. She is always neatly put together in a severe but nice way. While she is knitting she talks, and we listen to her.

Mother employs her to knit outfits for us girls. She has just knit woolen blue skirts and little jackets to complete the outfit for my sister and myself. Mother designed them to go with a blue and white checkered blouse with underwear of the same fabric. As soon as Teresita brings us the completed outfit, I put it on. I look at myself in our bedroom mirror. The mirror is an old one, with a gilded frame and black patches here and there. I guess the silver which was used in making these old mirrors is wearing out. The mirror is on top of the mahogany chest of drawers in my bedroom.

I look at myself in the mirror and can only see the upper part of my body. I have to stand on top of an armchair. I smile to myself, pleased at what I can see reflected in the mirror. Teresita's outfit fits me beautifully. I keep looking in the mirror, and it seems like it is the first time I'm seeing myself. Is that me? Next Sunday I know I am going to wear this new outfit to church.

Going to church is an important social event for us children. We get the chance to see and meet all of our and Mother's friends. Everybody is wearing the best dresses they own and look neat. We often attend the Holy Mass at the San Giovanni Battista Church, in Finalmarina. It is an outstanding baroque church with a white marble pulpit made by Bernini. It is a great piece of art, and I never get tired of looking at it. I hope God forgives me if often, instead of praying, I look at this harmonious piece of art, fascinated by the work of the sculptor.

The Sunday sermon is strictly religion, no politics, no nonsense. Mother finds it acceptable and refreshing, and I fully agree with her. After the Holy Mass we usually go to Ferro's Patisserie, which is located right in front of the Church. It is the place to go. On Sundays everyone notable in the village shows up for aperitifs or to buy patisserie for their Sunday lunches: the lawyer with his wife in Sunday clothes, the medical doctors (there are two of them in town), the pharmacist with a couple of his children and his wife, the sisters GR, famous spinsters who know everybody and everything that is happening. Eligible bachelors like Piero Acqua, who descends from good lineage and lives in his sister's mansion in the Finalmarina Central Square, come too. Just last year we would go to look at the incredible trays full of petit fours, the round almond cookies with the cherry in the middle, followed by a row of *cannoncini* filled with cream, then another row of small strawberry tarts, fresh croissants, an incredible assortment of fruit tarts, not to mention meringues with whipped cream. The smell of the patisserie would hit you as soon as you walked out of church.

Well, this morning after church Mother takes us to Ferro's "patisserie," but it is dramatically different. There's no sweet smell of the patisserie, only a strong smell of coffee, and not even real coffee but surrogate. The big, shining copper espresso machine stands idle, and the barman is making surrogate coffee with a little Neapolitan machine. Mother says that Orzo coffee is healthier, and she seeps it slowly and smiles that fabulous smile. I adore my mother. She looks so beautiful, and everybody admires her. I can see it when people come to greet her. I am so proud; I want so much to look and act like her.

• • •

In Finalpia, close to my school, there is a Benedictine Monastery where we often attend the Holy Mass, usually at ten o'clock, when the monks sing the Gregorian chants. This is the mass I deeply enjoy and feel in all my body and soul. I sit in the back of the altar among strangers, but I feel like I am alone with my emotions. When the mass is over I leave the church reluctantly, wishing it would last longer.

Chapter 8

Our days are full of the everyday routine. The war goes on, but the radio bulletins are not as frequent as before. The news is vague, the emphasis on the German troops conquering all of Europe. Even Russia is becoming a target for the master race, i.e. Hitler's Germany. The German/Russian campaign started well, but right now it seems to have reached a standstill. There are many casualties due to the severe Russian weather; the Italian military once again is badly equipped to stand up to the bitter, icy cold Russian winter. The situation is escalating to catastrophic proportions. This is not appearing on the news, but people are talking. They're very concerned. Napoleon Bonaparte suffered the same defeats that Hitler is suffering now.

Italy has another ally that no one talks about, the Japanese. At school the teacher never mentions the war, or for that matter politics. So I do not know what is happening around us in the world. I do not know anything about Japan except where it is geographically. I know little to nothing of its history or culture. I know that a couple of centuries ago, or maybe less, they isolated themselves from the rest of the world. (Later this fact would intrigue me quite a bit.) I know that an emperor rules Japan. I'm fascinated by different cultures, and the Japanese are definitely different. I don't think it's right that we're kept in the dark about Japan, because that is what it feels like. It is a feeling I do not particularly enjoy.

The Italian radio EIAR (*Ente Italiana Audizioni Radiofoniche*) doesn't mention our Japanese ally. We do not have any idea what is happening in the world. Does any other world exist besides ours? I sometimes wonder.

Often when we walk home from school we meet an elderly gentleman, Mr. Bosio, a friend of Mother's who always entertains us with pleasantries, then starts questioning us about our school, friends, and teachers. Before saying goodbye he never fails to add, "Books are good, you learn a lot from them, but remember to look around you. Nature is so perfect it will teach you plenty." He gently lifts his hat as a farewell gesture. I enjoy the brief encounters with him, and I am more attentive to my surroundings. I find myself pausing over a little green leaf, analyzing its texture, its color, its perfect shape. I feel bad when, after I hold it for a while in my hand, it withers. As long as it is on the plant it is alive, but if you cut it off, slowly the leaf dies. I think Mr. Bosio is right; nature is so perfect. I begin to see and appreciate those delicate wild flowers which grow in the open fields, and sometimes they flower at the borders of country roads, giving a gentle touch to the severity of the dark asphalt.

The evenings are long after dinner. Having finished my homework I get in the habit of reading books, sometimes even while soaking in the bathtub. It has become my favorite pastime. But this upsets Ernesta very much, because she wants to get me out to clean the tub. In order to save the hot water supply my sister and I usually share our evening bath.

One evening Mother makes a big announcement at the dinner table. "I bought a piece of land in Finalborgo which houses a beautiful vegetable garden, and I have employed a person named Gaggero to take care of it."

I am glad to hear this piece of news, but I feel sad because it means I cannot go to visit Sestimio. I ask Mother, "What about Sestimio?"

"Don't be concerned about him. This piece of land doesn't have fruit trees, and not the variety of veggies that Sestimio has. We will use him too, maybe a little bit less than before, but we'll still be his customer."

I enjoy her answer and feel better. I grew fond of Sestimio, and I would have been disappointed not to see him with his colorful produce. The next day, when we come back from school, Mother suggests we all go to see the new acquisition. So we all take off happily by bike: destination, Finalborgo. It takes us at least until four p.m. to reach the vegetable garden. "Take a left here," Mother says.

And here it is in front of us. It is a strip of land shaped like a big V. Along each side runs a country path. At the bottom of the V, almost hidden by green bushes, an old wooden door stands in front of us. I see Mother searching for something on top of the door. She is saying, "Gaggero told me that somewhere up here he hides the key." We all join her in the search. Once we find it, we are impressed by its size. Imagine an old iron key almost as big as my hand. The key hole of the old wooden door is also huge. I've never in my life seen something of these dimensions.

Mother gets hold of the monstrous rusted key. After many tentative tries, eventually the door opens. Hurray! We go in pushing each other, trying to be the first to enter. The plot is composed of terraces where the vegetables are neatly cultivated. A narrow stone stair on one side takes you to the terraces. I am pleasantly surprised by the beauty of this place. It is a harmony of green colors. I always thought vegetables were boring, but instead I look around at the terraces and the vegetable paths look neat and inviting.

There are baby zucchini topped by conical yellow flowers, green beans, peas, cucumbers, tomatoes, to say nothing of rosemary which grows in bushes, basil, parsley . . . this is a wonderful green paradise. We start picking the vegetables at random when we hear mother's voice. "Stop children, on the double."

"Why Mother, why?"

"I'll tell you why," Mother replies. "The man who is going to cultivate our vegetable garden doesn't want anyone picking the produce but himself."

"But why?" we keep asking her. "It is our garden after all, not his."

"Well," Mother says, "this is what he wants and I agreed." She adds, "He is the one who works the vegetable garden. We should be nice to him and respect his work."

We are not happy about this rule, but we obey. "Suppose when we come Gaggero is not around, what do we do?"

Mother says, "You will see, sooner or later he is going to show up." She is right as always. We see a man coming from the lateral path. Mother doesn't have to tell us who he is; we know it is Gaggero, the man who is going to take care of the vegetable garden. He is a medium-sized man, heavily built but not fat, his face of dark complexion, with a round red nose. But what dominates his features is a scar which runs from the left side of his lip nearly to his ear. He has dark, curly, uncombed hair around his neck and wears a red, checkered cotton neck scarf. We are a little surprised by his appearance. I think he looks like a pirate.

While Mother introduces us to Gaggero, we gather together and one by one shake hands with him. Then he proceeds to talk to Mother and never looks at us again. We see him picking the vegetables Mother asks for, and one by one he gently fills our baskets, placing them back on our bicycles. We happily go back home with our baskets full of fresh vegetables. I do not understand it, but the way back home always seems faster than the way there. When we get home, Ernesta is excited to see all the goodies. "At last," she says, "we can have vegetables with every meal." She is already planning the menu for dinner.

We are late and still have to do our homework, so we rush into the house as fast as we can. We race each other, and Mother scolds us for being too reckless and noisy. She tells us we have to be good examples to the other children.

It seems that these days we have a number of new things going on in our daily life. Mother announces that she was recently having a conversation with a gentleman who is selling a little house behind the recently purchased vegetable garden with an olive field. What fantastic news! Olive trees are my favorites. The hills surrounding our villages are all kept with olive groves. It is a sight impossible to forget. Olive trees for me are the most harmonious, powerful trees in the whole world.

Since I am an avid reader, I have already reread all my books at least twice. Often I sneak into Mother's room to get new books. Of course I am careful not to be caught red-handed. Mother wouldn't approve of my choices, I suppose. I'm sure she's probably right, but I cannot resist the temptation to hold and read books. Italian literature for young readers is limited; most are translated from foreign books, especially English, which has an extensive number of books for young adult readers. In Italy, when you are very young you read Collodi's *Pinocchio,* which is an enchanting tale about a wooden child who becomes human. The story in its simplicity has a moral component as well as an educational one. When I was very young I loved it and found it extremely amusing. Or you could read *Il Cuore* by De Amicis, *Il Giornalino di Gianburrasca,* or you read a weekly children's newspaper called *Il Corriere dei Piccoli.* When you're older you might read *Piccolo Mondo Antico,* which I have been reading for a while, but honestly it is so romantic, decadent, depressing... should I say more? Yes, I should add melancholic. The author wrote the book in 1885. I did like it, but it depressed me very much.

Alessandro Manzoni is considered one of the major Italian writers of all time. Born in 1785, he died in Milan in the year 1873. His mother, Giulia Beccaria, was a woman with a strong, domineering personality who had a great influence on her son's life and beliefs. Giulia (1738–1794) was the daughter of the famous criminal lawyer who wrote the essay on crime and punishment which played a major role in the abolishment of capital punishment and clemency in the Italian judiciary system. It is still enforced. Among other books, Manzoni wrote the famous *Promessi sposi,* a tragic epic novel in which he describes the life of his contemporaries. The main character is a powerful noble landlord who falls in love with a beautiful peasant girl, Lucia Mondella, who is betrothed to a young man employed by the nobleman. Lake Maggiore is the background of the unfolding events. The powerful noble is abusing his power. It's a dramatic novel where the power of the rich landowner and the vulnerability of the poor are emphasized.

I enjoyed reading Manzoni's *Promessi Sposi*. He has an incomparable skill with words, and his characters are regular human beings who one can relate to. The book is part of the curriculum of Italian schools. Some students hate him, since we have to learn some of the passages by heart.

Among the books I take from Mother's shelves there is one I enjoy the most—*The Chartreuse of Parma* by Stendhal. I am so fascinated by this wonderful book. The characters are so real and alive. I cannot put the book down. I read it while I am soaking in the bathtub or while I am in bed. This amazing novel captures my imagination so much it is becoming an obsession, I know it. But it is a pleasant obsession, so I indulge it. Fabrizio del Dongo is the main character in the book. He is a young, handsome nobleman growing up in Northern Italy in troubled times. He is surrounded by ladies from noble families who encourage his adventurous dreams. He leaves his protected life of leisure at his father's beautiful villa on Lake Maggiore to join Napoleon's campaign. I follow the historic events and the odyssey that Fabrizio goes through with trepidation. I share his feelings, his audacity, his honesty. I am deeply in love with him. I cannot believe one can fall in love with a character, but I can't help it.

The topic of my conversations with my sister nowadays is Fabrizio. "Del Dongo, Fabrizio," I say over and over. The sound of his name fills my heart with joy. It fills my soul and gives me a chill. This has never happened to me before. Rationally, to fall in love with a character in a book is unreal. I keep telling myself this over and over.

One night when my father is visiting, we are at the dinner table and I'm talking about Fabrizio Del Dongo with my sister, and I notice that Daddy is a little annoyed. After a while he looks at me and asks angrily, "Who is this Fabrizio? Stop talking about him." I am so terribly confused. Then, without lifting my head, I start giggling, and my sister Baby cannot hold herself any longer and bursts into a loud, uncontrolled laugh. She is good at that too. Daddy orders us to leave the table, and we obey.

Stendhal was born Marie Henry Beyle in Grenoble, France on January 23, 1783. At the age of seven his mother died. Her departure left a terrible mark on the young boy. Stendhal's father, a prominent and successful lawyer, didn't dedicate much of his time to the son. He was reared by a bitter, unmarried sister of his mother and by a strict Jesuit tutor, whose influence caused a stringent anticlericalism that he carried all his life. At sixteen Marie Henry left his native Grenoble for Paris to study mathematics at the Ecole Polytechnique. The next year he joined the Napoleon's army as an aide-de-camp.

Napoleon's campaign took him all over Europe: Russia,

Germany, Austria, and Italy. Stendhal was enthusiastic and very much interested in people, in art, and in history. And, if I may add, in women. During the campaign he diligently kept a diary of all the places he visited as well his love affairs. When the fall of Napoleon occurred in 1814, he left the army and settled in Milan, his favorite city.

There is a passage from *The Chartreuse of Parma* where he extols the virtues of the Italians. "Italian are sincere, honest people and if not intimidated will say what they think only intermittently." Stendhal installed himself happily in the city of Milan and found enjoyment, comfort, and amusement among the Milanese society. He was fascinated by the elegance, wit, and beauty of the young Italian noble ladies, so beautifully described in *The Chartreuse of Parma*. For the very first time in his life he had feelings of belonging.

In January of the year 1839, visiting friends in the beautiful city of Padua, Stendhal was presented with a journal narrating the life of the Duchess of Sanseverina written by a grand uncle of his host. Stendhal was so taken by this journal that he promised his friend and himself that they would write a novel based solely on the subject and characters of this journal. He lived among the Milanese by choice and felt like one of them. He was a great admirer of the Milanese ladies; he was enchanted by their simplicity, beauty, sophistication and charm. I am personally touched and proud that a talented writer like Stendhal chose my city as his dwelling place. I have read and reread so many chapters of this amazing novel and never get tired of it. I am enchanted by Stendhal's writing; it is music in my ears and in my soul. He has a wonderful gift for describing his characters, making them so life-like that they stay with the reader for a long time. For myself I must confess reading Stendhal has been an extraordinary experience. He is one of the greatest writers.

•••

For a while, every single night at exactly nine p.m., a British airplane scouts our sky. When it first happened at the beginning of the war you heard people screaming, "Enemy airplanes, take refuge!" Eventually we got used to this lonely excursionist and do not pay attention. The villagers named this RAF airplane "dirty Pippo." "It must be nine o'clock," they say when they hear the soft sound of this aircraft, which is quite different from the sound of the heavy bomber aircrafts. How quickly one learns these differences. Almost every night we wake up to the sound of the sirens announcing the enemy air raid.

The aircraft we hear now are bombers, recognizable by the heavy sound. They are probably going to bomb more important targets, but one never knows. So we get up from bed and run to the shelter.

At the thought that these airplanes could bomb children like us, I start praying. "Please God be sure that these bombs do not kill innocent people, please God." I press my hands against my stomach so hard that it hurts.

Our staff at home right now consists of Ernesta, our nanny, Luigia the chamber maid, and an elderly lady that Mother just employed as a cook. Her name is Mrs. Volpi. She is a local lady who keeps mostly to herself. Mother told us that she needed the work and a place to stay. That is all we know about her. I like her very much; she is so gentle and indeed quite a nice contrast with the other maids. One morning I wake up to the sound of heavy vehicles and loud foreign voices. Stunned, I get up from bed and peep out through the wooden shutters, and I see German soldiers in sidecars and military trucks carrying armaments. I run to Mother's room. My heart is beating fast. "Mother, the Germans are here."

"Yes," she says, "just do not open the windows for the time being." We do as Mother says.

Later in the day we learn that a German outpost is going to install itself at the hotel next door, which has been commandeered. The owner of the hotel is allowed to live there with his family.

In the beginning we do not look at the German soldiers while they are organizing their outpost. We pretend they are not there. I notice that they have horses, and I have never seen such big animals. I learn that they are Russian horses, cared for by Russian prisoners. A couple of times one of the Russian prisoners stops me just outside our main door while

I am going to school and addresses me in a broken German/Italian. He is a huge guy wearing a German military uniform. His jacket is not buttoned up properly, his hair is uncombed, his shoes untied . . . he looks sloppy and smells of horses.

I understand more or less what he is saying. In short, he tells me he is not a German, he is Russian, so he is my friend. Frankly I do not know where he gets this idea. "My name is Vassily. Vassily," and he hits his chest a couple of times to make sure I understand it is his name. I wish I could tell him that I am not dumb. I smile and keep going on my way. Mother tells us to be polite and go about our day, so I am doing that.

From our kitchen window we see the German soldiers walking around, smoking, laughing, reading newspapers, books or letters. Among the Germans, Vassily stands out for his height as well as for his baritone voice. The other Russian prisoners make a point of saying hello and trying to make conversation with us. One afternoon Vassily comes close to our window holding a balalaika and starts playing it. He plays well, and we are listening. After a while the other Russian prisoners join him and start dancing. They are great dancers. It is the first time we've seen this kind of music and dance, and we are fascinated. We applaud, and everybody is having a good time until we hear a whistle and the Russians take off.

Before this little musical interruption Vassily had been holding his instrument in his arms mocking the Italians by saying "Italians capitalists *spassiren* all the time no *arbeit*." I like Vassily but this is too much, and I make a face at him. He realizes I do not enjoy his pantomime, stops immediately, and starts playing his balalaika. I like him better when he plays his romantic songs than when he talks.

We do not really know what is happening in Russia, Germany, France, or Africa for that matter. Our universe is restricted to our family, school, and friends. The radio broadcast is controlled by the Fascist Government, and so are the newspapers, so the story is always the same. The Germans are conquering all of Europe; the enemy will be crushed by the Berlin/Rome/Tokyo axis. At night when I am trying to fall asleep, tossing in the cold sheets, I hear the German soldiers singing a tune which I guess is popular these days, "Lily Marlene Lily Marlene." They are probably drunk. The sound of their voices is raucous, monotonous, sad, and a little scary. I am frightened, but at the same time I am listening, fascinated by this sad melody. The German soldiers are very fond of this song, and it seems to me they sing it with broken hearts. When I wake up in the morning I forget the anxiety of the night and happily get up, ready to start the day.

One day we hear that Ernesta is going to Bergamo. Her home town is a little village not too far from the city, in Val Brembana I believe. She is going to attend her cousin's wedding. When I hear that I am surprised. Weddings in war time are rare, and in fact it turns out that the couple is not so young any more. After fifteen days she comes back, and she looks terrible. Her face which is often grey has dark circles around her eyes. She looks scarier than ever. We learn that the train she was traveling in was bombed on her way back from Bergamo. She stopped at our house in Milan and became the heroine of the day.

It just so happened, she tells us, that when she arrived at the house the gate was wide open, and in the driveway a couple of German cars were parked. Two German soldiers with their weapons were standing in front of the entrance. Ernesta, keeping her head down, managed to reach the garage in back of the house without being noticed. Once inside she saw that the Germans were searching through the house and saw my daddy talking to the German Officer. My father is quite fluent in the German language.

Ernesta noticed that Daddy seemed to be pleased to see her; consequently she decided to stay close to him. Indeed that was what Daddy expected her to do. At a certain moment the officer to whom my father was talking walked away to speak to his soldiers. Father got hold of Ernesta's arm and told her to go and fetch a locksmith. Immediately she took off in search of a locksmith. When she found one, she went running back to the house. Father directed both of them to go upstairs into the guest room, where hidden under a picture in the wall there was a safe. Daddy lost its key and remembered that inside he had an old revolver. Luckily, while the Germans were searching downstairs the locksmith managed to open the safe. Daddy fished out the revolver and gave it to Ernesta, who put it in her bag and quietly left the house, dumping the revolver into the Olona canal. I have to explain that the Germans were tipped off by some fascists who said that there were weapons hidden in our house. The Germans left the premises with all the wine from Daddy's cellar and a couple of antique tapestries. Even though Daddy felt the loss, he was still relieved that the Germans did not arrest him, or worse. For days Ernesta would entertain anyone who would listen to her with her great adventure with the Germans. After a while it got old, and even Ernesta got tired of it.

On March 15th, 1943 the Axis forces surrender in Africa. We do not hear this shocking news on our EIAR, which is the Italian Broadcast system. Lately this station is broadcasting mostly music all day long and into the night. We hear about the surrender of the axis troops from some friends who are connected with the resistance. No one, of course, is supposed to divulge the source of this news.

The same night we listen to the London broadcasting, "Tam tam tam: London calling." Here is Colonel Steven, and my heart starts beating fast. All of us are piled up in front of the small radio; we keep the volume low fearing someone will hear it. If you are caught listening to the London broadcast you can be arrested on the spot, and who knows what might happen to you. We learn that the British and Americans have defeated the German army in North Africa headed by Field

Marshal Rommel, the so-called desert fox. This is a big blow for the Germans, as well as for their allies.

Our daily life is almost normal. After a while one becomes conditioned to the environment, and what was not normal yesterday becomes normal today. What I am trying to say is that we accept and adapt to circumstances without a problem. It is amazing how fast one gets used to anything, either bad or good.

We are happy when we wake up in the morning, and we are alive and together.

We look out of the window and see that the Mediterranean Sea is still there, as are the palm trees in front of my window. We thank God for that, and try to go on with our lives.

The curfew keeps us locked in our houses at night. It starts at nine p.m. and ends at six a.m.

I must say we children enjoy playing hide and seek in the darkness of the house at night after dinner, and we really do not mind the curfew, especially in winter time. Mother lectures us every morning before going to school. "Make sure," she says, "not to talk politics." Politics? What are politics? we wonder. But we know what she is talking about. Do not comment about the war, the Germans, the Fascists. So, we try to comply with her requirement.

At night the air raids are getting more frequent and lasting longer. Now, before going to the shelter, Mother makes us wear under our T-shirts a corset in which have been sewn jewels and gold coins. I do not particularly enjoy wearing this bumpy corset, but I do understand that in case our house is bombed and destroyed at least we would have something to live on. We hear about so many people nowadays selling jewelry and gold coins to be able to support their families.

Every day I notice unusual happenings. The German soldiers don't spend time talking leisurely amongst themselves any more. There is no smoking, laughing, reading newspapers, or looking at the blue Mediterranean Sea. I watch them as much as I can during my free time. My window has a direct view of the German camp. I can see through the curtain, and they cannot see me. This gives me an exciting thrill. My favorite pastime nowadays is to keep an eye on the enemy. So far I have told no one about it.

I watch the soldiers wear their helmets and carry their rifles even when they are not on patrol duty. At night it seems to me the Germans are patrolling the empty streets more frequently than ever. I detect them by the sound of their boots on the street's asphalt. When I hear them, I hide cowardly under the pillow praying they will not come to collect us. I am afraid that someone might have reported us to the German authority for having listened to the London broadcast. I've heard that it has happened before. I lay still in my cold bed waiting anxiously for something, I am really not sure what, but I am afraid of something bad. We hear so many dreadful stories of people disappearing, being picked up by the Germans in the middle of the night. This is so very scary; I hug my pillow and fall asleep.

The Germans, our allies, are invading Italy. Even a little girl like me can see that. They are everywhere in full war gear. They preside over the key arteries of the country: airports, bridges, railway stations, highways, naval harbors. All this is quite disturbing. We are prisoners in our own country.

Chapter 9

One morning we are having breakfast, which consists of *caffe e latte* and a slice of wheat bread with apple jam (which I particularly dislike, but not having an alternative I spread a little of it on my bread). Mrs. Volpi is not around, but I do not find it unusual. Often in the morning she goes out shopping if something is missing or she hears that the store has an item available that she had been looking for for a long time. Ernesta is in charge. A few minutes later Mrs. Volpi shows up, her eyes red as if she has been crying. She is visibly agitated. My sister Baby and I exchange a worried look; has something happened that we do not know about? Mother shows up in the kitchen, which is quite unusual, and approaches Mrs. Volpi and tries to console her. She is getting worse and starts sobbing. Eventually she gets a hold of herself and says, "The Germans got my son."

A glacial silence falls on the room. Old and young, we all know how terrible it is to be taken by the Gestapo. We know, but we are not supposed to, that her son is the leader of the Communist party hiding in the mountains. These places where the partisans hide are difficult for the Germans to find. They move around constantly. But I guess he came to town, and the Gestapo caught him. What a tragedy! Maybe someone denounced him to the Germans; what a horrible deed.

    I go to school with a heavy heart, unable to concentrate on my work. I keep thinking about that poor boy. What is going to happen to him? It is difficult to follow the lesson. Everything seems so futile and unimportant compared to the tragedy of this young man. Time seems to stand still. I sit at my desk in class. My mind is disturbed by this morning's event. I am restless; I keep busy scribbling, and the pencil keeps breaking. What is the teacher talking about? I couldn't say. Finally the dismissing bell rings.

    I want to go home, and yet I am afraid to hear what's happening to Mrs. Volpi's son. Back from school, the house seems awfully quiet. I do not like it. Mother greets us with a smile, but when is she not smiling? She tells us to be quiet and do our homework, and she says "please understand."

    In the late afternoon we have two visitors; they come in and converse with Mother and Mrs. Volpi. The door of the kitchen is closed. Apparently these two guys belong to the same Communist cell as Mrs. Volpi's son, and they were hiding together up in the mountains. We learn that Volpi is being kept prisoner by the Germans next door. These comrades have a written message to be delivered to the prisoner, and they suggest Mrs. Volpi bring lunch to him tomorrow and hide the message in the food.

The same night, when Volpi's *compagni* left, we eat our dinner in silence. No one is able to make any conversation, because we are all very sad and concerned. After dinner I try to read my history book, but I cannot focus on the subject. It just doesn't make sense.

In bed I am tossing like never before. The sound of the German patrol boots pounds in unison with the beat of my heart. It is a scary feeling. I am frightened; I should go to Mother but I am paralyzed. I cannot get up. The night seems to never end. I hear all sorts of unfamiliar sounds, even voices. I wake up in the morning tired and unhappy. What happened to Mrs. Volpi's son?

We eat breakfast in silence. Reluctantly I join my sister going to school, my body and soul heavy with grief. I am sad, unhappy and outraged. The morning at school seems like it will never go by. I cannot concentrate. I see the teacher, but I do not have the faintest notion of what she says. Finally again the finishing bell rings, and we leave.

When we are back home from school at lunch time, Mrs. Volpi is in the kitchen preparing lunch for her son: pasta with tomato sauce, a slice of bread, cheese, and an apple. In silence we watch her; Mrs. Volpi is trying to hide the piece of paper with the *compagni's* message. Her hands are trembling. She tries to insert the paper into a loaf of bread. She fails, the bread breaks in two pieces, she picks another loaf and it happens again. She is frustrated and starts crying. It is heartbreaking for us to witness her grief and frustration. Mother tells her it is no use. Even if she manages to hide the piece of paper the Germans will find it, and then indeed we will be all in big trouble. Mrs. Volpi keeps weeping softly, her head bent over in despair. It is so painful to see her like this.

Mother makes her sit down, and while handing her a glass of water she says, "Do not worry. Gioietta is coming with you."

I am surprised to hear Mother says this, and I do not have time to react. Mrs. Volpi takes a large square napkin and wraps it around her son's meal. We are ready to go. Mother kisses me gently.

I am proud of the fact that Mother picks me to perform this difficult task. I am a little scared, not so sure of myself, so I try not to think. I walk straight with Mrs. Volpi at my side. She is carrying the meal like an infant in her arms. We get to the hotel's main entrance where two German soldiers are standing guard. They stop us cold. I point to the napkin containing the meal for the prisoner. I guess they understand or they are expecting us, because one of them escorts us inside the building.

Behind a desk in the narrow hall, a soldier is sitting. Without uttering a single word he takes hold of the meal. He puts it on the table and opens up the knot of the napkin and starts looking at the food. With a knife he dissects the bread and cuts the apple in two. I try not to look at Mrs. Volpi, but I feel that she is stiffing up, and so do I. After having examined the whole meal he hands it back and tells our escort to go ahead.

 He takes us down the hall, and with a kick of his boot opens the door. The room is pitch black. Coming from the daylight I cannot see a thing. I look again and see a person sitting against the wall. Mrs. Volpi sees him too. The person gets up and moves toward Mrs. Volpi quickly. I get hold of the meal while the two of them embrace. I try not to look at them, but I notice that the face of Mrs. Volpi's son is swollen; one eye is black and blue and you can hardly see his eye. I almost faint.

 Mrs. Volpi cannot hold back her grief anymore and starts crying. "Please, Mother," her son whispers. I get hold of Mrs. Volpi's arm. I squeeze it gently but as firmly as possible while I hand the meal to him. The German soldier gets hold of my arm and says "*Eraus*"—get out— in German. I do not know the language, but this I understand, especially with that tone of voice. Mrs. Volpi is so stunned by her grief that she cannot move. Once again I have to get hold of her arm and push her hard in order to get out of the room. I do not see what is going on. I just go to the main door and leave. The way back to the house is even faster than the way there.

 At home everyone is waiting, worried sick about us. They are relieved to see Mrs. Volpi and I back safe and sound. The look on Mrs. Volpi's face is upsetting, so no one asks questions about our delivery in front of her. We children and the grown-ups feel so inadequate not to be able to comfort her. It is horrible, and we know no one can do anything to help Mrs. Volpi's son. The only thing we can do is pray, so we do.

Two days later the same two *compagni* show up with the terrible news: Volpi and two others partisans have been executed by the Germans. What a terrible blow for all of us. What a cruelty; how could they commit such an act of violence against a human being? For God's sake, why do these awful, cruel things happen? Why, why, I keep asking myself.

It seems like a tornado went by us and left us unconscious. It is a nightmare; I am going to wake up tomorrow morning and everything is going to be like it was before.

Volpi is still in that dark room where we visited him just the day before yesterday. We are still in shock. I cannot get rid of this sadness which grabs my stomach. I run into the bathroom, lock the door (which I am not supposed to do) and start crying. I have been there for a long time when I hear a loud knocking at the door.

"Gioietta, what is wrong?" I open the bathroom door see Mother and start crying again. She takes me in her arms and gently caresses my head. It feels good. Slowly I calm down. I am not sobbing anymore.

It is so hard to forget this cruel terrible event. I cannot stand the sight of the German soldiers anymore. They are all murderers. Mother tries to distract us and often takes us and our friends for long walks. We stop sometimes at the patisserie for snacks, but unfortunately there are no more delicious petite fours, only disgusting cookies which taste of war. Anyway, I enjoy sitting at the patisserie. The round table where we are sipping our tea has a nice tablecloth. I like to look around to see who is here. Richeri Franco, the pharmacist, is sipping his espresso, chattering with friends. The wife of the physician is having a drink and gossiping with a lady friend.

July 25th, 1943. The war bulletin announces that General Badoglio has overthrown Mussolini's Government. King Vittorio Emanuele appoints General Pietro Badoglio Prime Minister. We are all in the dining room—us children, Mother, and the help—listening to the radio and trying to make some sense out of this new development.

Il Duce is sent into exile on the little island of Elba, the same island where Napoleon was exiled in 1814. Hearing this news, we look at each other in disbelief. Does this mean the war is over? My heart is acting up again and beating fast in my chest; is it joy? At last we are getting rid of these dumb fascists. It is the only way I can describe them. Surely this feeling will not last long. Close to me Ernesta is holding her head; she is actually crying. I always suspected she was in love with Mussolini.

There is a breeze outside, and from the open windows a

strong pungent scent of oleander invades our dining room. It is indeed a dramatic event which no one could foresee. The only thing we know about General Badoglio is that he drafted and executed the successful invasion of Ethiopia in 1935–36 and was hailed as a hero by Mussolini, who awarded him the title Duke of Addis Ababa. I heard lately something else about General Badoglio which is quite disturbing. Apparently while fighting the Ethiopians he used barbaric methods of repression. This fact has never been officially reported by the Fascist regime.

Our everyday life is changing dramatically; we are afraid to go places or speak to people. We are suspicious of everybody. It is a terrible way to live. The food stores are empty with no merchandise in the displays. Even on the black market, meat and poultry are seldom available. Ernesta makes tons of polenta, which is a thick maize-like porridge. One day she serves polenta with milk, the day after she fries it, other times she mixes it with tomato sauce and braises it in the oven. I must say I love polenta, however after the second or third meal of the same food, one gets a little tired and wishes to eat something else.

Another dish which is served these days is peas, the dry ones, which look like green flour. One day it appears on the table in the form of a soup, another day it is mixed with other veggies. But it is the same dry pea flour.

One morning Mrs. Volpi comes back from the market with a rabbit in her shopping bag. When we hear about it we all run to the kitchen to see the animal. She tells us that she met a friend who has a couple of rabbits for her own consumption who decided to sell her one of them. "Are we supposed to eat it?" we ask each other, puzzled.

Mrs. Volpi answers, "Of course, and with Ernesta's polenta it is going to be delicious, I assure you."

"Gross," my sister Baby says, and we all run out of the kitchen.

By the way, when the rabbit showed up cooked and served with polenta as a side dish it was welcomed by all. We ate it and all agreed it was a delicacy.

"We should thank God twice a day," Mother tells us. "Less fortunate people have only potatoes to eat if they are lucky." When Mother tells us this I feel guilty. The kids at Castel Franco come to my mind, and I ask Mother if I can bring them some of the dried peas and fresh veggies we have in the house. She says, "You go if you like. That it is indeed a good deed." And she kisses me gently. I diligently fill up my knapsack. Actually it is not mine; it belongs to my sister Lalla. It is made of red vinyl, and she uses it while she goes bicycling with her friends. But she is not here.

I am going to use Lalla's red knapsack, which makes me feel like a young lady. I fill it up with the food Mother gives me, and I take off. I climb up the long stone staircase which leads to Shanghai. Exhausted, I reach the top and am met by a horde of half-naked kids, and it seems to me that there are more in number than on that last visit I paid with my sisters long ago. I open my knapsack and distribute the food I brought with me. As soon as the kids get their packages they all suddenly disappear, leaving me all alone. I feel uneasy and a little surprised. I guess the kids were anxious to bring the stuff to their mothers. I descend to the village and go home.

My sister and I like to take long bicycle rides with our friends. We ride to the neighboring villages along the Mediterranean littoral. The Via Aurelia is empty of traffic for us to enjoy. These rides are so enchanting: the blue sky empty of clouds, a lovely sea breeze playing against my whole body. I feel happy. We sing and laugh at silly stories we make up. Then all of a sudden we meet a German convoy. We stop immediately and take refuge close to the wall. They go by us fast with their scary motorcycles and heavy military trucks.

In silence we turn back towards home. The sky is no longer blue, and the wind is cold, blowing from the sea inland. We are not chanting anymore. With our heads down we pedal as fast as we can. We want to go home.

September 8th, 1943. This date is engraved in my mind, soul, and body and will never fade away. The Italian radio is broadcasting the following war bulletin: the Badoglio's Government announces that an armistice with the Allied powers has been signed. Unfortunately, Badoglio's gang has neglected to declare war on Germany; consequently the Italian army is decimated without guidance. An army without a leader, what a disgrace. This is the worst thing which could happen to any army. What a terribly sad day for Italy and for all of us.

The next morning I wake up to an unfamiliar sound. At first I cannot identify it. I lift my head from the pillow in order to try to understand what this racket is about. For a second I think it is the rain. I get up from bed, lift the curtains, and look out of the window. A strong sun hits me; it is a clear, sunny September day. I hear the sound and cannot make it out. I listening carefully and realize it is the sound of steps hitting the asphalt. When I go out of the house on via Aurelia I see something which I am sure I will never be able to forget as long as I live.

A procession of men is walking in the middle of the street, dragging their feet.

They look like they have no strength to lift them. I know they are Italian soldiers because some of them are still wearing their uniforms. Others have civilian jackets with military pants; some are still carrying rifles.

I am shocked. Is this really happening?

These people walk in silence, dragging their feet, making that strange sound. When they halt they stare in front of them looking like walking ghosts. I am overwhelmed by this scene, confused and frightened. Without realizing it I am all of a sudden sobbing, unable to control myself. I put my hands on my face try to hide my emotion. I look around and see the rest of the villagers handing out civilian clothing. We give the men water and food. They do not stop walking, just grab the stuff and keep going. Where are they going? I do not believe they know, either. Most of these men are probably trying to reach their homes before the Germans get them. I know what that means: concentration camps in Germany or worse. Others I guess will try to join the partisans, hiding in the mountains to fight the Germans.

At night while I try to fall asleep I hear heavy trucks on the Aurelia road. In the dark of my room I pray. "God Please protect those poor soldiers. Hide them from the invaders, the cruel, frightening Germans." I am restless. I keep tossing in my bed. I have bad dreams; I still see the faces of those soldiers. I hear their boots hitting the asphalt, making that noise. I cover my ears with my hands trying to stop it, then, exasperated, I put my head under the pillow. I am listening to the sound of my sister breathing softly in her sleep. How can she sleep? I am asking myself how anyone can be able to sleep in times like this. I am tossing and turning, restless, until all of a sudden I fall into the soft arms of Orpheus.

CHAPTER 10

October 16th, 1943. Another war bulletin: General Badoglio's government and King Vittorio Emanuele III are fleeing to Brindisi to join the Allies. The Badoglio Government lasted about 52 days. The Germans, in the meantime, have liberated Mussolini, who forms the Republic of Salo, a puppet state backed by Nazi Germany. This event is deteriorating our way of life even more. Italy is divided not only physically, the north in the hands of the Germans and the south in the hands of the Anglo-Americans, but now the population is divided as well. One group sides with the Fascist *Republichini* (fighting with the Germans), while the others side the Partisans, and in the middle are the civilians, mainly old people, women, and children.

What a mess we are in, and it seems it's getting worse and worse by the day. The enemy air raids are more frequent, not only at night but during the day as well. We have to be ready all the time to take refuge. We are not allowed to wander around on our bicycles anymore. The autumn days are getting shorter; the wind from the sea is strong and cold. Big waves hit the shore with a threatening, rhythmic sound. It seems even nature is getting upset and cruel. When we go out, which is very seldom, we wear heavy jackets and woolen hats. Quite unusual, but necessary.

December 13th, 1943. It is early afternoon; we are playing cards at the dining room table.

Josephine Baker's record is playing in the gramophone. Her delicate voice sings, "*J'ai deux amours, mon Pay est Paris.*" We are fond of this record and play it often. The handle-operated gramophone is a *Voce del Padrone*. It is our only entertainment. I am particularly fond of it. I love to listen to records; I could spend all day listening, dreaming away while looking at the blue Mediterranean Sea. We have few records, and they're mostly in bad shape since we have been playing them over and over again. Unfortunately we cannot replace them, or for that matter buy other records, because there is no record store in Finalmarina.

The central window of the dining room, the one facing the Mediterranean Sea, is wide open. The December sun is not strong but warm enough to emanate a pleasant tepidness. I am looking out of the window while listening to Josephine Baker's song and I see the seawater shivering under a strong north wind. All of a sudden a loud blast echoes in the room, making the window glass tingle. We all get up from our seats and see in front of us two giant columns of water shooting up towards the blue winter sky: a fascinating sight. I think the enemies are attacking us. Meanwhile I see two parallel waves of water coming toward us. I am scared.

Outside I see the German soldiers running away, holding their rifles and trying to put their helmets on top of their heads. For a split second I almost laugh at them.

I realize immediately that the two columns of water are two torpedoes. I see them shining in the sun. Now they are traveling on top of the sand. I am motionless. I do not know what to do. Then, suddenly, the torpedoes stop.

"Let's get out fast!" I scream at the top of my lungs. In the hall we find Ernesta, her face like a ghost. She is frantically looking for Mario's shoe. "Forget it," I tell her, "just let's get out of here fast."

Now we are in the street, a bunch of frightened kids. We join the "brave" German soldiers looking for shelter. In front of the main entrance of our house there is a villa built after World War I, which is surrounded by a medium-size wall. We all take shelter there.

The morning after, a procession of villagers comes to see the two shining torpedoes lying on the beach like two giant whales belly up. Among the visitors animated discussions are endless; each one of them has his own opinion about this event. It seems they all agree that an English submarine torpedoed a German barge full of war armament. Some of that cargo is spattered all around the beach. It seems like a population of rotten debris. To me the torpedoes look like monsters.

The barge wreckage lays there in the shallow water for as long as I can remember. It becomes like a landmark. The village photographer, Mr. Regis, who is the father of one of my new best friends, Renata, takes great snapshots of the torpedoes as well as of the sunken German barge. He exhibits them in the window of his store in the Finalmarina main square for a long period, well after the war was over.

A couple of days after this event the German authorities make us evacuate the premises. Mother rents a villa half a mile from our own house. The owner is an engineer who works for the Piaggio aircraft manufacturers who has been transferred to another post. The house is bigger than ours and has a great garden, and we have neighbors! The other villa on the left belongs to some friend of Mother's, the Crivelli family, industrialists from Milan, but it is empty right now. On the right the lovely Genovese villa belongs to the Castelbarcos, also good friends of Mother's.

I am happy to move to another location. I was growing somewhat paranoid seeing those German soldiers so close to us. Thank God once again.

The wife of the owner of the villa we are renting is an American lady who left behind a ton of *Collier* magazines, which I discover the first day of our arrival. These magazines are piled up in the otherwise empty closet of the room mother assigns to my sister and me. "This is the best discovery since Christopher Colombus discovered America," I solemnly declare to my sister.

I am literally fascinated by the images and photos in *Collier* magazine. I could spend all day long looking at them, and I'll tell you, I did. This is making Ernesta upset with me. I really do not care, and I spend as much time as I want going through the amazing pages of this interesting magazine. I have never seen anything like it. I sit on the floor and start looking at the beautiful photographs. I am fascinated by a photo of autumn scenery, with big, fabulous trees. Some have red leaves, another has golden yellow leaves. "Autumn in New England" they say. Even if I don't know the English language, I guess it. "I thought England was in Europe," I think to myself. It's confusing; I have to learn this language fast if I want to know what the articles say.

Beautiful girls wear pretty clothes, white knee socks and loafers. I wish so much to look like them. I wear my hair parted in the middle with two pig tails, but I change my hairdo often. I am famous for being versatile in my appearance. It is my way of expressing myself.

In the morning I am late for breakfast, late for school, then late for snack and late for dinner, and why? Well, I am busy studying and looking and trying to understand English, which I do not know. "I am going to learn this language," I keep telling myself. It is a must.

We are only residing in the villa for a couple of days when

we learn that the Crivelli's house has been commandeered by the Germans to be their headquarters. Just our luck! The commander of this post happens to be a noble German, not a nobleman, a Von something . . . I never remember his name. Anyway, Mother says she met him, and he seems a decent man who tried to speak to her in fairly comprehensible French.

In the backyard of the villa we rented there is a deep grotto carved in the mountain that we are using as air raid shelter. We find out that our friends, the Richeris, whose father is the local pharmacist, are staying with our next-door neighbors, the Castelbarcos. We are going to share the same shelter. This is extremely good news for us kids; at least we have friends around.

The grotto is now being furnished with wooden bunks which will be our sleeping quarters during the enemy's night air raids. I am excited and look forward to spending the nights there. No more getting up in the middle of night for us. Around midnight Mother often organized a late supper consisting of a delicious risotto alla Milanese, served at the entrance of the grotto on a long wooden table. The monotonous sound of the grass hoppers keeps us company while we eat the delicious risotto. The war and its horrors are forgotten. We try to be as quiet as possible, because we do not want to be heard by the Germans next door. It is not easy with our exuberance.

During the days we go to school, and we try not to wonder about too much. We play in the garden close to the grotto just in case an air raid comes during the day. When we stroll on Saturdays or Sundays along the Viale Delle Palme promenade between Finalpia and Finalmarina, I note that very few young people are around. Girls walk together in groups, gossiping, pretending not to see the boys or hear their flattering comments. The promenade stroll is a must for young people and adults as well.

Many young men are disappearing; I assume they are joining the partisans in the mountains.

We have a lot of time on our hands. We are attending school intermittently, and air raids are frequent, even during the day. We are forced to stay home, close to the shelter. On Sunday, the Prior of the Benedictine Convent comes to the Castelbarco's to celebrate the Holy Mass in the garden. We all attend, and before Mass the Prior sits on a chair and, one by one, he hears our confessions. When my turn comes I am a little embarrassed to stand in front of him and tell him all of my mischievous acts. It is hard, and I am not so good, and I try to remember how many sins I have been committing. Sometimes I cannot think of anything bad or improper I've done, so I improvise . . . I improvise something, but I am panicking. What do I tell him? He probably understands my effort, and he gives me absolution and tells me to recite four Ave Maria's for penitence for the sins I do not remember.

When I tire of looking at the *Collier* magazines, I pick up my Stendhal, *The Chartreuse de Parme,* which I cleverly cover with the newspaper so it looks like my textbooks. All school textbooks are covered with newspaper to protect them from use and abuse. I feel so good about myself for having had the idea to cover the Stendhal book like the other school books so no one will know what kind of book I am reading. Regular wrapping paper is hard to find, but we have plenty of newspaper in the house because Mother buys the *Corriere della Sera* daily.

Speaking of paper, one that is no longer available is toilet paper. One of my tasks is to cut the newspaper into small square pieces to be placed in the bathrooms. It's my duty to supply. I miss the toilet paper, but even so I am aware that in a time of war you can't be too fussy. I guess one can get used to anything, especially if there are no alternatives.

The members of the Richeri family are becoming our closest friends. Franco, the pharmacist, is a delightful, helpful gentleman who dedicates his life to his profession. People rely on him, and I understand why. He is honest and trustworthy, and when I visit the pharmacy with my sister he lets us go in the back while he is preparing the potions for his patients. He treats us to licorice, which I learn is one of the ingredients often used when mixing the cough medicine. The pharmacist's role is so vital. God forbid we cause him to make a small mistake. We are aware of that and keep quiet, just observing.

The pharmacy is located in an old three-story building off the Finalmarina main square with high arched ceilings. The walls have shelves with old pharmaceutical potteries. Franco wears a white smock, which I think is quite becoming. He is always busy, and yet he always greets us with a smile. His friendly welcome makes us very happy indeed. We feel important and appreciated, which doesn't happen often. Everybody in town knows him as among the town's elite, together with the medical doctors, the mayor, and the local poet Gianduaia.

Franco is married to a charming lady, the Marchesa Vival Di Pasqua, from an old aristocratic family. Marco Vival Di Pasqua, Duke of San Giovanni, "Great" of Spain, and count of Casabianca of Luceto, just to name a few of his titles, was her father. Since the year 1292 the Vivaldi Pasqua were famous Commanders of the great Genovese Fleet. One of these noble men tried to reach India via the Cape of Good Hope. Another Vivaldi Pasqua, Giovanni, was one of the founders in Genoa of the "Banco San Giorgio," a powerful financial institution in the fifteenth century. Another Vivaldi P. is mentioned in the records. He was elected Doge of the Republic of Genoa from 1556 to 1558. All of these famous, eminent noblemen of the past made the name Vivaldi Pasqua important even in our time.

Marco Vival Di Pasqua joined the Italian Royal Navy at an early age and left it at the end of World War I. He then started his own business in boat salvaging in the harbor of

Savona. The Marco Vivaldi Pasqua family took residence in the resort town of Finalmarina in 1920. Marco was an expert sailor and owned a slick cutter. During the summer he loved sailing on the sparkling Mediterranean Sea. He is the founder of the Finalmarina Nautical Club. Franco Richeri married Marco Vival Di Pasqua's daughter, Maria Luisa, called Memi, in 1938. We met Franco and his family in 1940, the first year of war. Of course now that they reside in the Castelbarco's villa next to our new residence, we've become good friends. Franco and his wife Memi have two children—Giuseppe, called Eppe, and Tussi. My sister and I take these two kids under our protection.

Since our move, we attend classes in a new school in Finalmarina. We make new friends. The girls are nice and fairly good students as well. This fact makes me more competitive, and I try to do my best in all of the subjects. The teachers at school are nuns; they are quite strict but fair, supportive of our work and attentive to our comments. I am surprised and happy when I discover this. Our classroom is a cheerful, spacious room with two large windows letting in the sunshine, and the soft, fresh spring breeze putting everybody in a cheerful mood.

One morning Mother Superior is coming to visit our class to announce the appointment of a new religion teacher. She says his name is Father Salvatore Graziani, a Military Chaplain of the Benedictine Friars. I am happy to hear this news since I am very fond of the Benedictine order. However, I am a little uneasy since Don Salvatore is the nephew of a famous Fascist General, Rodolfo Graziani. Don Salvatore comes from the Monastery in Finalpia, where my family often attends Sunday Mass. I am as great admirer of the Benedictine order that lives there and their philosophy of life. The monks wake up at dawn to pray and read the Psalms prior to celebrating Mass and then spend the day working in the fields.

The ten o'clock Mass is my favorite one, since the Mass is celebrated with the Gregorian Chants. I could sit there in the cantor pew forever; the Gregorian Chants have a profound effect on me. I feel relaxed, peaceful, and content. It is so mystical—I am so happy there.

The new religion teacher shows up in our classroom escorted by Mother Superior. Don Salvatore is handsome in his long Benedictine robe, which gives him a majestic look. He is smiling, showing his perfect white teeth. The entire class gets up to greet him. He introduces himself then sits at the teacher's desk, fixing his long black tunic. He makes sure it falls properly in place. He opens the attendance book and proceeds to call our names. When we get up he asks a couple of questions, then with a motion of his hand he signals us to sit back down. The religion class goes by fast, though no religious topic has been discussed so far. He is trying to charm us with his witty remarks about life in general. I already dislike him a little bit. It's just a feeling—I might be proven wrong. It seems to me he's trying too hard to please the class. I wonder why.

At Christmas my sister and I each receive a pair of roller skates. We are delighted, and we practice all day long along Via Aurelia, which is practically empty of traffic. Once in a while a bicycle crosses our path, or horse-driven carts, or German motorcycles, all looking at us with curiosity. Pretty soon I master the skill of roller skating. I'm enjoying myself; it is exhilarating to go faster and faster.

One morning my sister and I decide to roller-skate to school. It is amazing how fast we get there. Our arrival provokes quite a commotion among our fellow students. They circle around us in admiration, and we feel like a million dollars to have an audience. But it doesn't last long, because Mother Superior shows up to check on this unusual assembly in front of the school's main entrance. She looks at both my sister and me with a stern look and says, "What on earth are these devilish devices you have on?" We are so shocked by her remark that we do not answer, trying not to laugh. Mother Superior adds, "Everybody to class, the bell is going to ring in a minute, hurry up." She leaves and keeps saying, "It is not acceptable, it is not. What are they going to invent next?"

After that first day that we roller-skated to school, we take the precaution of taking the skates off before entering school grounds and hide them under our coats on the hanging rack in the school's vestibule. Mother Superior never came back to check on us.

I like the nuns, but there is one that I like the most, Suor

Margherita. She is beautiful, outspoken, friendly, and easy to talk to. We become good friends, and I know I can trust her. It's a nice feeling to have a grown-up who understands and respects me. Suor Margherita is a wonderful human being, and I am sincerely fond of her.

My favorite girl friend is Renata Regis, daughter of the photographer who has a store in the Finalmarina main square. She is a vivacious brunette, keeps her hair short, has an olive complexion, perfect white teeth, and a luminous smile. She's a pleasure to be with, and we bond right away. We're real friends; we like to study together, gossip, bicycle, laugh, and just plain have fun.

A couple of times we skip classes and go to the movies. The first time we did that it went well, but the second time a friend of my mother's happened to be in the same theater and told Mother she saw us. I got in trouble, but Renata didn't because she didn't know the woman. Lucky girl!

Chapter 11

One afternoon, having finished my homework rather quickly, I'm pondering how to spend my free time in a productive way, asking myself over and over what I could do. After a while I come up with the idea to start a newspaper. What do I know about how to start a newspaper? I do not even own a typewriter. As an avid reader as well as listener of the radio, especially the BBC London broadcast "Colonel Stevens calling from London," I was up to date on current events. I share the idea with my sister Baby. She agrees that it would be a great way to spread the news to our friends. We are very wrapped up with this project; it gives us so much to think about. I don't have a clear concept of how it's possible to make this dream of ours come true. The only thing I am sure of is my determination to do it. A newspaper . . . I cannot believe I have such a daring project. Yes, it feels good, but how can I realize this? This is the big challenge. I have to prove to myself that I can do it. I make a list in order to figure out what I need, but it's not so easy. Actually, it's difficult. Where do I start? Paper seems to be essential, but paper is not easily available these days, even stationery paper. What am I to do?

Well, I can use the sheets from my exercise books. One problem is solved, now what should I call it? I like "*Il Gazzettino*," even though I know it is a common name for a newspaper. It is difficult to find a suitable name for my paper; it would probably be wise not to name it. I take a sheet from my new exercise book and start to write the front page. I put the date on the right and then the title of the first article.

I have many brilliant thoughts on what to write but find it difficult to focus on one subject. I should listen to the London broadcast in order to write some up-to-date news. So I go to listen, but my bad luck, they are announcing brief messages like "the fruit is ripe," "the night is cold," "the moon is full." I try to interpret these codes. I am sure the English airplanes are dropping food and war deterrents to the partisans and are giving them the instructions. So I deduce that the partisans are getting help from the British in the fight against the Germans. The drop is probably during the full moon. I am writing an essay in which I give the information I learn as well as gossip I hear.

Then I went out to get the time table of the coach service which connects the villages. This coach is actually drawn by a horse. It is called *tramballero* because the ride is bumpy. It's used by passengers who commute from one village to the other. I spend almost half an hour locating the operator of the coach, to no avail. I have been standing here at this stop for quite a while. Other people are waiting as well, so I ask whether they know at what time the coach is coming. "No, we do not have any idea, but we wait."

Another half an hour goes by, and then we see the *tramballero* coming around the curve and approaching the stop. It stops, and people flock in. The coach is simple, rectangular in shape with three rows of five seats each, maybe six if the sixth is a child. Along the sides of the coach a rail protects the passengers. On top is a canvas to protect from the rain. I direct my attention to the driver and try to get some information from him, like the locations of the stops and the time table. I write down his more or less clear information in my notebook. The passengers are upset because the coach is not moving, and they are complaining loudly. I am finished with my interview, and to the relief of all the passengers the *tramballero* takes off.

I go back home none too satisfied, but at least I have some information which will allow me to write about the coach: where it goes, where it stops, and when it runs. I am a little bit tired and, let's say, frustrated. I still have to figure out the layout of my newspaper. I've become a bit more realistic and decide to call it a newsletter. I feel good about this, and the more I think about it, the happier I am. I know what a newspaper looks like, I even like its smell, but I doubt I can do that. I was dreaming, and I guess I have to admit that I enjoyed dreaming about it.

I write my article on the coach, giving as much information as I can. However, I cannot assure my readers about the reliability of the service. I write the essay with my best handwriting, but when I finish the page I notice that on the first half of the page my handwriting is constant, while on the second half it tends to be different. I have to rewrite the piece paying more attention to how I write, which is not an easy task. In the end I'm pleased with my accomplishment.

In order to make my newsletter worth reading, I am well aware I should write more up-to-date news. I need to write more compelling stories. I am young but I do understand the time we are living in is not an easy one, for any of us. The war, the politics, the fight between the fascists and the partisans, not to mention the Germans . . . talking about it is dangerous enough, writing is even more dangerous, though tempting. For the time being I am going to play it safe. I will list the names of the stores that still carry merchandise!

Another thing I can do and am doing is give my readers useful information. I take my bike and make the rounds for my newsletter. The first stop is the main Church in Finalmarina, San Giovanni Battista, where I get the Holy Mass schedule. On the way back home I stop at the Finalpia Benedictine Church where I copy the Holy Mass hours into my notebook. This information will be listed with the rest in the newsletter. I am mighty proud of my work. I look at the newsletter and like what I have done. Since it has many pages it looks kind of loose, so I get a needle and stitch the pages together. For the final touch I tie on a red ribbon to better hold the pages together.

I show my sister the finished product. She takes the newsletter in her hand, looks through it, then looks at me with a big smile and says, "Not bad, not bad indeed!" Her remark makes my day. We are now ready to deliver the newsletter to our customers, who are of course our friends and neighbors. At this point we realize we have not thought how much we should charge our customers for the newsletter. What a dilemma, should we charge our readers or not? And if we charge them, how much would be the right amount?

We spend a lot of time discussing what to do. The news is produced and delivered by us.

"It must have a price," I keep thinking, "it must."

In the end I settle it by giving it for free, and for the next edition I will decide how much to charge. The first copy goes to Mother; we hand it to her with some trepidation, because her reaction is so important. Mother says, "I have to admit I'm impressed by the work you have done in putting together this newsletter, good job, and I should add it is not an easy task to accomplish all by yourselves," and she embraces both of us. Mother's approval of our project makes me happy. Now I am thinking the big challenge for Baby and me is to produce this newsletter weekly.

Chapter 12

One breezy January morning the wind comes from the east. The Mediterranean Sea, usually crystalline blue, is black with big waves hitting the shore. We have to wear heavy windbreakers and gloves. The village is deserted. My sister and I hurry on our skates to reach school. We keep our heads down in order to protect us from the cold wind which hits our faces, making our eyes water and our noses run. We get to school just in time. The first class of the morning is religion, and Don Salvatore is already sitting at his desk ready to start his class. I sit down at my desk and try to listen to what the teacher is talking about, but I am distracted. I cannot concentrate, and I follow my own thoughts. I'm aware, however, that Don Salvatore is looking at me. He knows I am not listening to him, and sure enough he says, "Gioietta, are you with us this morning or is the wind taking you away from us?" The entire class bursts into a roaring laugh.

I do not answer and try to listen just in case Don Salvatore asks me a question about the lesson. I do not have the faintest idea what he is talking about, but I get it when he says, "So as I said before, it is the duty of a citizen to denounce to the Authority the whereabouts of the partisans."

I am so shook up by this sentence that I cannot utter a word. I look at Renata and almost start screaming, "This is outrageous! A spiritual leader should not say such blasphemy." I think he's a dirty fascist. I knew it. I knew it.

Don Salvatore gets up from his seat and looks at me, his face red with anger, his eyes seem to pop out of their sockets, his voice is raucous. "What are you saying? What are you saying?"

I am speechless. I tend to lose my voice when I am crossed. I am frightened; he is coming too close to me. Is he going to hit me? I am afraid. I feel his rage hitting my body. Then in the complete silence of the classroom I hear him saying, "This is not going to end here." The dismissal bell rings, and all the students disappear quickly.

I am still upset. Don Salvatore passes by me and seems not to see me. I bravely manage to look at him, but he turns his head and leaves the classroom. "I am sure he is going to report me to Mother Superior," I tell Renata while we gather our books before leaving the classroom. My sister and I both leave school very upset, not exchanging a word. Finally when we reach home I ask her, "Should I tell Mother?" She says, "Maybe you should." But I am a coward and do not say anything. At night alone in my cold bed I toss restlessly. I am scared. I am terribly afraid of Don Salvatore's reaction to my comments. Is he going to denounce my family to the Fascists? They will come to arrest us and take all of us who knows where. Maybe he saw my newsletter and is going to the authorities showing my news about the London broadcast. Oh, am I in big trouble. It is my own fault if this is going to happen. Never in my whole life have I been so afraid. It is my fault; why have I been so silly? It is too late now. "I knew it," I keep repeating to myself over and over again. Exhausted, I fall asleep, but I am not resting peacefully.

In the morning I wake up late and tired. Everybody is already having breakfast. No one seems to notice my worries. My sister Baby is upset at my lateness. We manage to recoup the time by zooming to school on our roller skates as fast as we can. We actually get there a couple of minutes before the starting bell. During the morning break I go to look for Suor Margherita, my favorite nun. I decide to share with her my problem with Don Salvatore. I look all over for her, and finally I meet her in the vestibule. She is busy chatting with another nun. I look at her, she acknowledges my presence by smiling at me, and adds, "Anything I can do for you, Gioietta?"

"Yes," I say. "May I speak with you, please?" She cuts short her conversation with the nun and turns her attention to me. At first I am a little hesitant, not knowing how to tell her what happened between myself and my religion teacher. I clear my throat, and start to spill the beans. "I made Don

Salvatore violently mad at me during his religion class."

"So?" she answers, "I do not think you should worry about it."

"Wait," I tell her, "until I tell you what happened. You will change your mind for sure." I proceed to tell her: "During Don Salvatore's class yesterday morning I was not really attentive. I noticed that he was looking at me, so I started paying attention to what he was saying." I quote, "It is the duty of a citizen to denounce to the authorities the whereabouts of the partisans." I am trembling, but I manage to tell Suor Margherita my response to Don Salvatore's assertion. "He got very upset at my reaction, and I feared he was going to strike me in front of the entire class. I was lucky the dismissing bell rang. Don Salvatore walked out of the class room murmuring, 'it is not finished here, I warn you.'"

Suor Marguerite is in a complete state of shock. Her face is purple and very cross. She looks at me bewildered, finally saying, "Tell me, Gioietta, that is not true, that you made it up." But Suor Margherita knows I would not be able to fabricate such an awful story. She then adds, "You know Gioietta I always thought Don Salvatore was vain, but I didn't know he was such an unspeakable character. Do not be afraid; he is not going to mention this to Mother Superior, otherwise he is the one who is going to be in big trouble, not you my dear." I am so happy and relieved hearing her comment that I feel like kissing her. Instead I say thank you and go back to class.

I thought the case was closed for good. Instead when Baby and I go back home, Mother summons me to her room and asks me why I behaved badly in religion class the other day. "How do you know?" I ask her.

"Well," she says, "Don Salvatore paid me a visit this morning while you were at school. He was complaining about your behavior towards him in class. He sounded upset with you."

"Did he tell you why I was not behaving like he would like me to?"

"I do not recall," she tells me.

"See, I'll tell you, Mother. Don Salvatore is a dirty fascist if there ever was one." Mother is upset at my outburst.

"Please calm down and tell me the facts."

"Gladly," I say, and I quote to her the sentence which made me furious. She too is visibly upset upon hearing Don Salvatore's remark. She pauses for a while and then tells me not to tell anyone about this unfortunate incident, adding, "with Don Salvatore behave like nothing has happened."

After this unfortunate argument with Don Salvatore, I become very close to Suor Margherita. We often meet during recess and have lively conversations, even though she does most of the talking. She tells me that in life it is important to take care of your body as well as your mind. "*Mens sana in corpore sano*," should be everyone's motto. I listen to her carefully, then I question her on how I can take care of my mind . . . it is so abstract. Taking care of the body I understand: exercise and eating well takes care of that, but the mind is a little bit more complex. She smiles and says, "read good books, be interested in the world, in people, study, pray, meditate."

"God, how can I do all these?" I ask her.

"Well," she answers, "it is not easy. The best you can do is try."

Back from school, I tell Mother what Suor Margherita told me. "Suor Margherita is right, it is important to take care of your body and mind. For your body it is important to exercise and keep clean. In life you have to try to control yourself, which is why the mind is important. You have to cultivate your mind, and knowledge is the nourishment of the mind."

"How do you achieve knowledge?"

"Well," Mother says, "you study and read good books, books that teach you about life, behavior, religion and so on."

I am overwhelmed. Mother detects my confusion and embraces me, saying, "Do not worry, you are lucky to have someone who cares about you and teaches you all that."

I have been reading a book I found on Mother's bookshelves. This book was written by a Swedish gymnast in which she explains how healthy it is if one exercises daily. The book is complete with photos of each exercise. Fitness is the key to staying young and beautiful. This is the message the author tries to convey to the reader. It is working on me; for days I read the book, study the photos demonstrating the positions and movements of each exercise diligently. Now I am ready to start this fitness program.

I am trying to follow all the instructions as carefully as possible. My sister Baby is looking at me while I exercise, and from the expression on her face I detect that she thinks I am cuckoo. For a while I diligently perform these exercises, then one day I forget my Swedish gymnastic drills and go back to the usual routine of my day.

However, I make up my mind to change my hair style. My dream is to gather my hair in back in a big braid like those beautiful Nordic girls whose names are like Ingrid or Viveka. Well, it's a nice thought. The texture of my hair is terribly fine and slippery, so it's very hard to look like those girls! When, with difficulty, I braid my hair, it looks so unappealing! It has no volume. It looks bad to say the least. I say goodbye. For the last time I look at myself in the mirror, undo my hair, and forget all about it. I close this chapter on my Nordic look.

Chapter 13

One August day during the summer of 1944, everything is hot: the sun, the wind, the air, the grass, the oleanders, the fig tree, and the asphalt on the streets. We children are confined to the house. It is dangerous to venture outside. The Germans next door are restless, cars coming in and out of their driveway. Dispatchers are in full war gear, hurrying up and down in a carousel. I spy on them from the bushes which separate our garden from theirs. My head is spinning; there is so much going on. At home everything is quiet. Mother is reading in the living room, while Ernesta and the others help in the kitchen, gossiping as usual.

Baby and I know it is strictly forbidden to go to the beach. Lately the English aircrafts are coming during the day to shell German troops in transit. We all know this, but we do not really care. We decide it is time to go for a swim in the sea. In order to reach the shore we have to cross our street and the next one, which is the Via Aurelia, a sure target for the British planes. We sneak out of the garden, look around, and see no one, so we proceed with caution towards the beach. The white sand is shining under the forceful August sun. The empty beach looks strange to me. We plunge into the sea, and it feels so good. We swim, dive, splash, and laugh. How wonderful to be in the water at last. Baby and I are swimming happily in the empty Mediterranean Sea like little mermaids, singing, splashing, and diving in the cool water.

All of a sudden I hear the sound of an airplane approaching. I am scared; I do not know what to do. My first instinct tells me to get out of the water and run. I understand that it is far too late, too dangerous; the airplanes with their scary roar are on top of us and start shooting with their machine guns. God, we are being punished for disobeying Mother's orders. What do we do? I duck and swim under water as long as I can. When I surface I look at my sister, also surfacing. Her eyes are so big and scared. I tell her, "Let's get out of here." The enemy airplanes are gone as fast as they came. We rush back to the house.

We meet no one—the streets are deserted. As soon as we get to the house we are greeted by Ernesta scolding us, saying they could not find us anywhere and got terribly worried. I promise her I will never go swimming as long as the war lasts. I had my share and am still shaking. It is hard to describe what one feels when something like that happens to you. You die for a split second, and then it is over, forgotten. Did it really happen?

One afternoon I am going to the newsstand to see if any newspapers are available, and I meet in the street one of my classmates, Renata Regis. She whispers into my ear, "Did you hear about that guy who came in by train in a casket?"

"What?" I retort. "What do you mean, a living person in a casket, are you kidding me?"

"No, believe me, it is true. Everybody knows it, it is the latest news in town, trust me."

She looks at me; I look at her and burst into a loud laugh.

I would like to know more about this unusual hot piece of information. I learn from different sources that this guy, the one who arrived in the casket, is rumored to be a major *capataz* in the Fascist entourage. And he comes from a province in the center of Italy. It seems also that he's a good medical doctor. Everyone has a different version of this unusual event, which, by the way, reminds me of a short story by Gogol (one of my favorite authors).

One afternoon school closed early. When we arrive home, we find Ernesta in the kitchen. I ask her for a glass of fresh squeezed orange juice, but she replies, "I'm afraid I do not have time for you children, because la Signora is expecting Miss Caviglia for tea."

"Big deal," I'm thinking. I do not understand what all the fuss is about.

"Do you know who Miss Caviglia is?" Ernesta asks me.

"So what?" I say. "She is the daughter of General Caviglia, Italian Field Marshall Enrico Caviglia, Finalmarina 1862–1945. I know that after September 8th, 1943 General Caviglia, self-appointed Chief of the City of Rome, negotiated the surrender of Rome to the German Army. General Caviglia was successful in persuading the Germans and the Allies to declare Rome an open city. I am proud of him. This agreement has proven to be a wise choice, and the entire world will be forever grateful to General Enrico Caviglia and his committee for having saved the eternal city from destruction."

When I finish my speech I see that Ernesta is quite impressed and doesn't add anything, keeping herself busy in the kitchen, but . . . she does not squeeze the oranges.

Miss Caviglia shows up at four o'clock sharp, wearing an elegant white and blue printed silk dress, her dark, gently waived hair pulled up into a chignon. She smells good; I recognize the Chanel No. 5 that Mother also uses. I am standing in the kitchen with the door partly open and can see what is happening in the vestibule. When Mother greets Mrs. Piera Caviglia Franzinis I retreat back in order to keep an eye on Ernesta, while pretending to be busy with my homework at the kitchen table. I notice that, after shining the Victorian tea set, Ernesta places the Bohemian tea cups on the silver tray, covered by a starched white linen napkin. I am impressed at how elegant the tray looks. Surely Mother had something to do with it. I always liked that tea set with the delicate white color of the porcelain. The china is such a perfectly transparent white that I can see myself mirrored in it. I hold the cup; it's feather light. Ernesta gives me a dirty look, so I put it immediately back in its place.

Mother still has some English tea she has been saving for a long time. I see Ernesta warming up the tea pot by pouring boiling water in, letting it sit for a while, pouring it out, and then putting three spoons of tea leaves into the bottom of the warmed tea pot. One teaspoon for each person, and one for the pot, she tells me as she pours more boiling water into the teapot. Then she fixes her organdy apron and leaves the kitchen with the tea tray. A second later she is back, having forgotten the little dish with the small canapés she managed to put together: a slice of tomato and a drop of olive oil on a small, dark piece of bread that she has put on a pretty dish of the same pattern as my favorite tea set. I count the canapés; there are six of them, and they look good. While she left the canapé dish on the kitchen counter I was tempted to snatch one, but they are so well displayed that I'm afraid Ernesta would notice it right away. I decide to be a good girl for once, resisting the temptation. I am, however, restless. I wish I could hear what the two ladies are saying.

After probably half an hour, the door of the living room opens up, and I see Mother and her guest going towards the door. I am lucky; for a while I can see this famous lady in full light. I know she lived in Rome for a long time, mingling with the high Fascist rank. Mussolini's daughter, Edda Ciano, was one of her closest friends, along with many other celebrities of the time . . . the life of the ruling class. How exciting it must have been. After spending many glamorous years in swinging Rome, Miss Caviglia came back to Finalmarina to marry a handsome engineer who worked at the Piaggio factory.

A couple of months went by, and one day we hear that General Caviglia's daughter, Piera, is dead. I am shocked. How could this be possible? I saw her with my own eyes! She was just here visiting Mother, when was that, a few months ago, maybe less? I am literally speechless. I am not able to understand. We learn that one night Miss Caviglia was not feeling well, so she went to bed with one of those electric blankets, which probably was defective. Apparently she fell asleep and burned to death. How horrible.

There is a lot of gossip going around town on this subject. The latest I hear is that the lady in question was a morphine addict, and that's really how she died: from an overdose. I am not very familiar with what it means to be addicted to morphine, but one of my older friends explains to me that it is a kind of medication prescribed to terminally ill patients to alleviate their suffering. But it seems that some like to use it as an escape from every day life.

I don't understand why someone wants to escape from everyday life. Even wartime, as scary as it is, is worth living through. There is always someone who needs you, and every single morning when I wake up a new hope fills my heart, and I thank God I am alive.

Rumor has it that pretty soon the partisans are coming out of hiding to fight the Germans in the streets. Night and day, heavy traffic is heard on the Aurelia. I wonder if the Germans are leaving and where they're going. The Anglo American troops are coming; it seems to me there is little escape from them.

We stay home after school, playing in the yard, restless as we spy on the Germans next door. The nighttime air raids seem to have stopped; there is actually more action during the day. In fact, the air raids now are mostly aimed at the evacuating German troops. The milk lady brings news with her delivery as well. All the men of the village, young and old, are gone to join the resistance. Food delivery is sporadic. Then she rushes off like someone is chasing her.

We go to school every morning on our skates and sit in the classroom, but no one is paying much attention to what is going on in the class, not the students or the teachers. It's a great relief when the dismissing bell rings. We rush home, afraid of having missed something. What we might miss we do not know, but we rush home as soon as the bell rings.

These days we seldom hear from Daddy. We know he is fine, and so is Lalla. The war bulletins are getting shorter every day: enemy attacks, air raids, warning us not to talk and to stay home, etc.

Chapter 14

The year is 1945, the fifth year of war. Our daily life is getting complicated to say the least. It seems a long time since the Anglo American allies invaded Sicily. It is taking an awfully long time for them to reach the northern part of Italy. The Germans are staging a desperate resistance to the allied army. Our country is divided by the war and in terrible shape. The Germans treat us like their enemies, not their allies. The main cities have been bombed and suffered heavy casualties among the civilians. Most of the men, young and old, have been deported to Germany or are hiding in the mountains. Our country is in bad shape, and it hurts. We civilians are oppressed and cannot defend ourselves, especially being a population of women, children, and the elderly. The Germans and the Fascists are on one side of the street, and on the other side, hidden up in the mountains, are the Communists, Socialists, Liberals, Christian Democrats, and Monarchists . . . all united in fighting the Germans. Some families are divided by their political beliefs.

Fortunately, the number of so-called *Repubblichini*, the Fascist followers of Mussolini after his liberation, seems to be a minority, even though they are very loud. It is even harder to be neutral. It is a bloody mess. I look at the people around me, and I see fear in their faces. It's hard to live when anything can happen to you at any time, anywhere. More and more, however, I see and feel that everybody wants to get rid of the Germans. This determination is easy to detect. No word is said, but everybody knows; it is only a matter of time before we will get rid of them. The Germans know it too. The war has changed course. No more German supremacy; the war bulletin doesn't say much these days. The German Empire is trembling and crumbling, and we hear it loud and clear. "Tam, tam, tam: London is calling." Colonel Stevenson is sending coded messages to the resistance all day and long into the night. We know something big is going to happen. "The fruit is ripe," the voice on the radio keeps saying again and again. But when is it going to happen?

The Germans next door seem busier than ever. I position myself at one side of our garden where I can easily see the main entrance and see a German soldier standing on guard in full combat gear. Dispatchers go in and out of the driveway, arriving or leaving on their motorcycles. It's like a procession. Once in a while a military vehicle pulls in, and a high ranking officer comes out. I recognize him as such because of his elegant uniform, which makes him stand out among the other soldiers. He is handsome and severe looking. All the soldiers freeze while he marches into the entrance of the headquarters and disappears from my sight. Too bad, I wish I could see what is happening inside.

Recently, I have not seen the captain who is in charge of the German outpost next door. He came to pay a visit to Mother a while back. We kind of like him; he has always been proper and polite with us. I wonder what is happening to him. I remember that a couple of times I've heard the sound of the London broadcast coming through his office window. Maybe Von-something is in trouble with the SS for listening to the London broadcasts.

I'm not scared, but I feel the fever rising around me, and I'm getting excited and restless. I know that something is going to happen soon, to all of us. We live our lives day by day. At night the curfew seems to start earlier and earlier. The streets are empty, and a strange silence embraces us. Once in a while the silence is broken by a sniper. We fear the Germans are attacking the civilians, or the partisans are attacking the German soldiers. I do not dare to think what is going to happen next.

People seem speechless when they meet in the street, I notice. They stare at each other in silence and keep on their own way. No one trusts anyone else. It's a strange feeling; there are no words to be found in times like we're experiencing. No time for chit chat, nothing good to share with one another, fear of a horrible event about to happen to all of us. What is going to happen when the Germans leave, I wonder. Where are the Americans?

Lately Mother is quiet. She spends most of the day reading in her room. She probably misses her beautiful house, her close friends, and Daddy.

Chapter 15

One early spring morning the windows of our classroom are wide open, and the smell of spring is invading the room as well as the students. I am sitting at my desk with my books in front of me, but my mind is elsewhere when a knock at the door wakes me up. A nun comes in, whispers something to the teacher, and leaves.

"Gioietta and Baby," says the teacher, "please come here." My sister and I approach the teacher's desk. "A lady outside wants to speak to both of you." I am surprised. We both step out of the classroom and see Pina, the caretaker of the house, standing in the vestibule. She is visibly upset when she sees us, and she says, "Come home right away. Mrs. Calori fell from her bicycle. Dr. Franco said you have to come home immediately."

I'm so upset that I start running. I know Baby is following me. I do not see her, but I hear her panting as we dash out of the classroom as fast as possible. We put on our skates and off we go. The way home has never seemed so long. We get home and Mother is sitting in an armchair in the shaded living room. The curtains have not been drawn. She looks different. I am frightened and try to hold myself, but I start crying. I do not know why, but I'm scared to see her sitting there. She doesn't seem herself. I feel a pain gripping my stomach.

Mother quietly tells us that the doctor wants her to go to Savona to be admitted to the hospital. Apparently she fainted and fell while riding her bicycle. It must have been a gentle fall; she doesn't have any visible bruises. I am worried. "Why did this happen, why, why?" I cannot stop asking myself over and over again. I cannot find an answer. I am confused and unprepared for this event, which touches me deeply. I am lost. What a mystery is a human being?

The hospital is located about forty-five miles from our house, in the city of Savona. Private citizens are not allowed to use their cars, and besides, where can one find the gasoline to operate a car? A car and a driver are provided by General Caviglia to take Mother to the hospital. I pray, "God, please help her, please, I will be a good girl, I promise, I promise." When the car comes to pick Mother up I am standing in front of the door, and I do not want to let Mother go. If only I can get into the car with her it would be so different. I will protect her. I know I can make her better with my loving care. Mother enters the car, the door closes, and the car leaves. I want to run after the car screaming, "Stop, stop, wait for me, I want to come with you, please wait!" Instead I am standing there watching the car, which in a split second disappears from my sight.

I am upset, confused, and terribly cross with the entire world. My whole body is trembling with rage. I cannot cry. I go into the house and run upstairs into my bedroom and start to cry at last. I lay in bed, unable to stop crying. I guess I fall asleep. I don't know how long I lie there. When I hear someone come in I open my eyes and see Ernesta gently touch my arm. "Dinner is ready, please come."

What is she talking about? How can I eat while Mother is on her way to the hospital? I look at her like I've never seen her before in my life. She feels my despair and quietly leaves the room. I am touched and grateful for her understanding and respect for my grief.

I believe that Franco Richeri called Daddy on the phone in Milan, and Lalla will go to Savona to assist Mother. I would have liked to go with her, but who would be with my sister Gabriella and the others? I am left with Baby, Dominic, and Mario Jr., who is, at nine years old, a well-behaved boy. Ernesta is handling him beautifully. He is the sweetest boy you would ever meet, intelligent and always behaving like a little gentleman. He's a pleasure to have around. The oldest one, Dominic, is seventeen and not so easy to handle, to say the least. At fifteen, I am in charge even though no one ever puts me in this position. I feel responsible since no one else is here with us kids. My sister Baby follows me like a shadow.

I feel good having her close to me; her presence gives me strength.

Everything seems to be at a standstill. Often we do not attend class due to all of the uncertainties. I cannot grasp the fact that, just a couple of days ago, my life was so easy and even cheerful, with no worries, no pain. I didn't mind the war, the German occupation, the air raids, the curfew and all those other discomforts we had to suffer. All that, indeed, was nothing compared to what is happening now. I wish I could go back.

A couple of mornings after Mother left for the hospital, my brother Dominic doesn't show up at the breakfast table. Ernesta runs upstairs to check his room and comes back with the news that not only is he not there, he didn't even sleep in his bed. This is really terrible, what on earth is happening? I am scared, lonely, and confused. Our world is indeed falling apart. We're in shock: speechless, confused. I cannot figure out what is happening. Worse, I do not know what to think, what to do. At least Mother is not here to witness it. That thought doesn't cheer me up either.

It worries me that I am alone with my siblings and no one to talk to. I am confused and unprepared to face all of these traumatic events. It is not the best time of my young life; it is a nightmare. Sometimes I ask myself what is really happening to me.

And yet, life goes on. We wake up in the morning, eat breakfast, go to school, come back, do our homework, have dinner, and go to bed again. For a while we do not hear anything from the hospital. I am so worried I do not know what to do or what to think. One day, out of the blue, someone comes to the house with a message that Mother is recuperating from her operation, and my sister Lalla is with her. We learn also that it took her three days to reach Savona from Milan. Poor Lalla, it must have been hell. What an odyssey for a young lady to go through. It is a relief to hear about the operation, but I am still deeply concerned about Mother. The worries are many, too much, and too overwhelming for me.

While Mother is away at the hospital I stay home and try to cope with the everyday events. I feel lonely; where is everybody when I need help, direction, and support? I am sitting at the table while we eat dinner. Just a couple of days ago we were sitting at the same table, having such a good time, Mother presiding over us with her cheerful smile, emanating warmth and much-needed confidence. I always wanted to be like her. Now is the time to try to emulate her. So I look around the table and smile timidly. They all look quite okay. Mario Jr. is eating, making Ernesta happy. Gabriella is also busy eating; she enjoys good food. I try to eat, but the food doesn't appeal to me. I am thinking about Mother and Dominic, where he is right now.

That night at the grotto shelter, Franco tells me he got a call from Daddy saying that Dominic got to Milan safely after a trip of several days. It is not clear how he travelled and how he managed in these difficult times. We do not get many details, but at least I know he is safe. That is what counts. At last some decent news! I thank God for that.

Once in a while I still find the time to monitor our next door neighbors, the ugly German soldiers, from my observatory. What a different view from a week ago. No soldier is guarding the entrance. The premises look deserted, with just a couple of military trucks at the end of the driveway . . . ready to take off, I guess. The German soldiers are packing up. They load the army trucks with their ammunitions, rifles, uniforms, gas masks, helmets, and cases of wine. I even saw them loading motorcycles. I wonder why they do not drive them. Probably they do not have enough gasoline. How can I rejoice when my heart is heavy? I am worried and confused.

At night, and sometimes during the day too, we hear the sound of sniper shots. We close all the windows tight, and we stay clear of them. Some of the windows have shutters, and these are kept closed at all times. The house is dark, sad, and scary. In times like this anything can happen; we all know that.

The milk lady sometimes comes late and sometimes doesn't show up for days. When she reappears she leaves the bottles at the door and runs quickly away. No more gossip, just fear. We miss the latest news and gossip that she used to deliver with the daily milk. We spend the nights in the shelter, where the Richeri family is taking refuge, too. No more games of hide and seek in the garden, no more risotto at midnight, no more laughter and silly jokes about the fascist bravado. I see how tense and nervous the people around us seem, so preoccupied they are almost absent. We stick together, afraid something is going to happen. We spend most of the time in the shelter or nearby. It is not advisable to go into the streets, which are awfully empty. Once in a while I do venture to the entrance of our house to try to see what is happening outside. Everything seems so very still under the sparkling April sun.

I miss Mother very much, but I do not dare say it to anyone. I am lost without her. Franco tells us that he heard the Americans are at last making their way north. "What does that mean?" I ask him.

"It means the war is soon going to be over, my dear little girl."

I guess this is exciting news. After five long years the war is going to be over. We have been waiting for this day for five long, miserable years. I am supposed to rejoice and be happy; the war is going to be over soon, so they say. I am so astonished at not being able to enjoy this wonderful event. "Be happy," they all say, "sing, the war is going to be over soon, very soon, do you understand?" I try to smile but cannot. I have a pain in my stomach. It hurts badly. My heart is heavy with grief. Mother is at the hospital still, how can I enjoy this moment? I am upset because no one understands the pain I feel. I try to say something, but my voice is trembling and I start sobbing. Memi Richerdi tries to comfort me. "She is coming home soon, you will see," she says. I get a hold of myself, a little embarrassed about showing my emotions, and try to smile softly.

A couple of days later, early in the morning I venture out of the shelter onto the deserted street. I see a tall man with a rifle and a red scarf around his neck who screams at me, "Get home, get away fast! It is dangerous!" He has not yet finished his sentence and I have already retreated to the garden and into the house, shutting the door tight.

A couple of minutes later I hear an exchange of gunshots. I run and hide in the closet, trembling a little. I feel my face burning, I hear voices and come out of the closet. "Oh here you are." Ernesta urges us to stay put far away from the windows. Good, I think, this is the first time she's made sense.

We are all hiding in the same closet, and needless to say we do not fit. I run upstairs into my room and hide under the bed. I hear gunfire. Are they going to come in and kill us? Are they? God, please help us, I know I am not good, but I promise I am going to be so good. I close my eyes. Maybe nothing is happening. I am trying to convince myself

Then I hear voices, gunshots, people screaming. I hear someone running. I wonder if they are the partisans chasing the fascists. Oh God, I am scared. My legs feel feeble. What am I supposed to do? Run, but where? Certainly I should tell everybody to stay away from the windows, even though we've already closed the wooden shutters. "Everybody under the bed!" I scream, "quick, quick!" I burst into hysterical laughter, but I guess no one notices it. Everyone is so busy running for shelter under the beds, where else?

Meanwhile, outside the fight in the streets is getting louder. I am so tense my whole body is tight, like a violin string waiting for something terrible to happen. I've heard that there is a group of fascists in town, and I know the partisans are fighting them. Why are they killing each other? We are all brothers and sisters, all Italians. What is it, are we all going mad? Where does all this hate for each other come from? I do not get it. Is it power? Probably I am too young to understand politics, but to me it is pure stupidity. Though I might be able to understand fighting the enemy, especially the Germans, who have proven so cruel and ruthless. I hear more gunshots echoing all around us, together with the dry sound of machine guns. It is scary and confusing. I hold my hands so tightly that it hurts. I am surprised how all the kids are holding up; probably they really do not understand what is going on outside.

All of a sudden the gunfire stops. The silence that follows is scarier. Sure enough, a big blast goes off that seems close to our street. The sound of the explosion is not ending, but actually increasing fast. Again we hear more gunshots. They are fighting in the streets. The man I saw, I'm sure, was a partisan, a Communist according to his red scarf. I was quite impressed by his strong, tall body, handsome face, and long, blond hair falling on his red scarf. He was carrying a rifle, or maybe it was a machine gun under his right arm. I saw him briefly, but his image is clearly impressed in my mind. I am praying for his safety. I honestly don't want anyone to get hurt, please God.

After a while we are back in the dining room with the windows shut tight. No light comes through; it is getting dark. It is almost seven o'clock, time for dinner. I hear the familiar sound from the kitchen of supper being prepared. There's still gun fire, but it seems very far away, so we resume our routine, taking our evening baths, putting on our pajamas, and going to dinner. I am surprised that Ernesta manages to put together a decent meal considering that no one was able to go to the store in the last couple of days, but she makes vegetable soup with pastina, slices of polenta, and a small portion of cheese which we divide equally. There seems to be no fighting; maybe we are all a little too scared.

Before putting Mario Jr. to bed, Ernesta urges us to go to bed right away and pray to God for the safety of our family and friends. I think this is very decent, and I assure her that we will. I run upstairs into the bedroom I share with my sister and start praying. It has indeed been a long, scary day for all of us.

I thought I would be able to fall asleep easily, but once again I prove myself wrong. I lay with my head straight up on the pillow, my arms folded under my neck, motionless, attentive. I know if I move I am bound to miss something vital. I wish Mother was here with us to give us support and direction. Just her presence would change things, I know. I hear the hurried sound of steps, voices as well, singing and coming down the street below my bedroom window, even though they do not face the street directly, with the garden between my room and the street. There are more gunshots, some seem closer than others, and I am still trying to figure out who is firing these shots. The house is quiet, with no sound whatsoever. Probably after a day like today everybody is sound asleep. I pray for Mother to come back recovered, for Daddy, for Dominic. I hope Mother doesn't know about his disappearance. It is all so terribly complicated why all these things happen together. I keep wondering why. It is very hard for me to comprehend. Maybe it's not happening and I'm just making up all these events in my mind. I am tired; my imagination is playing tricks on me. It is so unusual for a positive person like myself to think this way. I realize how much I miss my mother's support, her radiant smile, her love, her presence. I always picture myself as a strong, cheerful, optimistic human being. What's happening to me? "Please God help us to go through this trying time. I do not know what to do or even think. I promise you I will be a good girl. I promise I will never disobey Mother or tell lies again. I will never make fun of Ernesta or any other inferior person. I will be patient with my sisters and brothers. I hereby solemnly swear."

I feel tired. Exhausted. My mouth is dry but I'm too scared

to go downstairs to the kitchen to get a glass of water. My head and eyes are getting heavier and heavier. I close my eyes and grotesque faces of men and women, all screaming, appear in front of me. I am scared. I cover my face with my hands, but it doesn't help. In the bed close to mine my sister Baby is sound asleep. Her peaceful sleep reassures me, however I wish I too would fall asleep. Sure enough, after a while it seems my wish has been granted, and gradually, without realizing it, I join her in a deep sleep.

Chapter 16

April 25th, 1945. I wake up to the sound of thousands of church bells ringing in the clear spring morning, a joyous sound which makes me leap out of bed. War must be over. It is clear. The church bells announce the end of our suffering. Thank God for that.

The sun is coming into my room through the shutters, so it must be late. The joyous sound of the church bells makes everything around my room look happy and sharp. I have never noticed before how lovely my bedroom is. The sound is solemn, and the bells do not stop ringing. I hear chanting voices coming up from the streets in a crescendo, like water boiling on the stove. I jump out of the bed, wake up my sister, and we both run down the stairs in our pajamas. We are both so eager to go out and be part of this historical event that we get dressed, forget breakfast, and out the door we go. Church bells are echoing around us on the sunny April day. The streets are full of people everywhere; it is quite a scene. We are used to empty streets with a few people bicycling and once in a while our beloved *tramballero* going by. It is quite a surprise now.

In the kitchen we hear that someone has reported that the Americans are coming. At last the war will be over. There will be no more fighting, no more air raids, no more hiding and suffering. Hurray, Hurray!

As soon as we cross our street we meet something amazing: a horde of people of all ages. Young men and women carry riffles around their shoulders, sporting bright red scarves around their necks. They march along the street chanting, "*Bandiera Rossa trionfera,*" the official Communist hymn. Red flags are everywhere, a cheerful crowd indeed. I look around, but I do not recognize any one. The older ones carry children on their shoulders in order to protect them, or protect themselves. They are all chanting and screaming. I am looking at this amazing gathering in astonishment. "Is this really happening?" I ask myself.

Everybody is so relieved they're letting go. Some are crying with the news, some are embracing one another. There is dancing, chanting "*Bandiera rossa.*" It is like an explosion, those five long years of repression and at last freedom is here. I look around and I see so many young boys, probably my age, carrying rifles like trophies with big smiles on their young faces. Big trucks are filled with young men standing in the back of the vehicles, their long hair and red scarves flying, each carrying a rifle. These trucks cruise through the village, and the crowd cheers when they pass by.

I am wondering where all these people are coming from. My head is spinning, everybody is singing *Bandiera Rossa*, clapping, calling each other, kissing, dancing, and screaming "we made it!" Victory at last. These are the young and old people that, for almost five years, have been in hiding in the hills fighting the German army. Some of them lived in caves up in the remote part of the mountains where no one would live, changing their location all the time in order not to be captured by the German army. Many young people never came back, dead in combat or in the concentration or labor camps in Germany, our ex allies.

I know for a fact that much sabotage against the German troops has been carried out by the partisans. So many of them lost their young lives, and so many civilians as well. Today is truly their day to celebrate victory. Today is the day for them to show their faces to the world. The partisans are triumphant in their own right. I cheer with them. They deserve our thanks and support for their fight and bravery.

As soon as we approach the street leading to the main square of the village we see an oceanic crowd all carrying the red flags with the communist emblem of the hammer and sickle, "*falce e Martello*." I see a myriad of flying red flags, the breeze from the Mediterranean Sea fills them up and they look like giant red balloons. It is indeed an impressive sight; young, middle age, old men and women are all out to celebrate the end of war, the end of suffering the end of oppression the end of abuse and injustice. Hurray!

I am pleasantly excited. All these exultant people with their screaming and chanting have deeply influenced my sister and me. We start embracing, chanting and dancing in circles with those close to us. Never in my whole life have I seen such a large, loud crowd. It is a little intimidating, I must confess. My sister and I are holding hands and trying to stick together, afraid to be divided. And we try as well to stay to the side of the main stream. The crowd now is swelling; it seems that people are now running toward the main square, which is at the end of the promenade. Someone screams, "They got them, the dirty *bagasce*, the traitors. . . . " My sister and I try to make sense of the insults and to whom they are directed. Even if we do not want to go, we are literally transported by the people around us. After a while we find ourselves in the main square together with many other screaming people. We are getting quite scared. The faces around us are no longer happy faces. They are angry, screaming insults and making terrible threats. I notice that the women are more violent than the men.

What we see now is quite shocking. In the middle of the square, on a couple of chairs (the kind you find in churches), stands a group of four or five young girls with their dresses all ripped up, their faces black and blue, evidently having been badly beaten. Some of the girls are crying softly like little kittens, others just stare in front of them, horrified, looking like empty bodies. The crowd is screaming all sorts of obscenities directed at the girls. Some people try to get hold of them, but luckily a team of five armed partisans intervene and succeed in holding them back. "Bastards, traitors, good for nothing . . ."

A lady spectator like us whispers, "Those are the girls that went with the German soldiers during the occupation." It is pandemonium. I am confused. I cannot believe this is happening. I feel my face burning as if I have a high fever. I do not know if this is caused by my rage or my fear. All around us everyone, especially the women, are screaming their hearts out. "Traitors, whores," and more unspeakable insults in a crescendo. There is so much hate, so much resentment, exploding all at once.

My sister and I are frightened and try to stay as close as possible to each other. One of the partisans who probably, by her looks, is the chief, gets hold of one of the young girls and starts to cut her hair. The girl starts crying. Even from where we are standing I can see tears coming down her cheeks. When she is finished cutting, she gets a razor and shaves the young girl's head. Oh God, what is she doing? I look at my sister in disbelief, and I see fear in her eyes. The crowd around us is cheering, screaming insults towards these unfortunate girls. I am ashamed of what I am witnessing. I want to disappear. The people are pushing us, and I am afraid of losing my sister. I am afraid they are going to beat us up.

My sister and I cannot stand this unspeakable act of violence against these poor girls. I am shivering, unable to articulate. I want to scream, "Stop! Stop!" but no sound comes out from my mouth, which is dry. I am so upset, outraged with myself for not being able to do something to prevent this terrible act of violence against these poor defenseless girls. Why is no one speaking up? Are we all such cowards?

I am ashamed and guilty for not being able to do something to stop this cruelty.

We try to go back home but it is not easy. The crowd is so thick it is hard to break through. We are panicking, and we feel trapped. What a scary feeling, what a nightmare. I am holding back my tears while we try to get through the incredibly wild behavior of this screaming crowd. The mob seems to be completely out of control. We are horrified seeing the hate spilling out, transforming these people into killers. They are ready to kill. We understand no one is going to stop them, we know that, we feel that.

It is difficult for us to move an inch either forward or backward. We are transported, swept away. It is like when you are swimming in the ocean and the current takes you; there's little we can do to prevent it. It is the most horrible feeling one can experience. We are afraid to be separated. The mob is so compact and so angry my sister and I hold each other together as tightly as possible. My hands hurt badly I'm holding Baby's arm so hard. We feel trapped; we do not see a way to escape this mob.

Desperate as we are, abruptly we turn around and find ourselves on the parallel street to the Aurelia, which is less crowded with people. We are now able to move a little more freely, thank God, and we proceed toward our house. Soon we are home! Home at last! The windows are closed, and the outside pandemonium is muffled. Thank God once again. Now that we are safe at home my fears have kind of disappeared. We sit down at the kitchen table, drained, not able to tell what we saw in the Finalmarina's main square. What an ordeal; I am still shaky and disturbed. It is beyond my belief, even beyond my comprehension. How can one be so cruel and cold blooded like those women in the mob? I cannot believe the cruel violence I witnessed just moments ago, which is probably still going on. Frankly I cannot image what these women are able to inflict on those unfortunate girls. I am trembling, and I feel guilty for running away, for not having the courage to scream something, to stop the horrible act of violence, at these defenseless human beings. Shame one me. I am deeply hurt and upset. How can someone do anything like that in cold blood? Are we all so bad, so cruel, so merciless? Shame, shame on us all. What do we know about the circumstances which led them to fraternize with the German soldiers? Maybe they were forced to keep company with the enemy. These girls deserve a trial like any other human being. I am angry with myself for not standing up and for behaving like a coward. To witness such a cruel act is so traumatic, therefore I find it extremely difficult to talk about it. I just choke. I am sitting here with my emotions, unable to articulate them. What really struck me most was that the women were more violent than the men. They seem to compete among themselves in their anger.

Ernesta tells us that someone told her that a team of partisans got hold of a couple of fascists and killed them on the spot. I choose not to believe it. I am lucky, indeed, not to have seen that execution. I pretend I have to go to the bathroom to be able to cry at last. I have probably been in there for longer than I think when I hear a knock at the door. "Are you all right?" says Ernesta. I quickly dry my eyes and come out sporting a broad smile. There are no questions asked. Good, I do not have to answer.

All night we hear chanting and the like. We do not dare to go out, but even so I am tempted to do so. But common sense tells me I better wait for the morning. So I do stay home trying to listen to the radio broadcast which airs *Bandiera rossa* speeches of the various Communist, Socialists, and Democratic leaders, all proclaiming their victory. In the morning when we come down to breakfast, we hear that many outrageous episodes of violence have been committed by yesterday's mob. My sister and I look at each other, aware that something awful could have happened. We sit in silence, keeping our heads down, trying to forget what we experienced. I am glad that the war is over at last, hard as it has been to believe it. No more air raids, no more fighting in the streets, no more killings, no more curfews, no more German soldiers dominating and terrorizing us . . . I thank you God with all my heart. Yes, at last we will be a united family, Daddy, Mother, Lalla, Dominic, Baby, Mario, and myself.

CHAPTER 17

My sister Lalla calls the Richeri Pharmacy from the hospital and apparently speaks to our friend Franco, announcing that Mother is recovering well. Lalla adds that soon probably we will take her back home. I look up when I hear this news. I say "Thank you God so very much." For me this is the best news ever, even better than the liberation. I am happy, so happy. It is hard for me to stay still.

I am jumping out of my skin. There are no words to describe my happiness. I am crying for joy. I feel so good. How much I've missed mother . . . I have no words.

At home we are all overwhelmed with joy that mother is coming back at last. The events of the last days right now seem of no importance to me. Someone comes to pay a visit and announces that the Americans are in town. Out of curiosity, my sister and I go out to see what these Americans look like. Well, as soon as we enter the via Aurelia we see heavy traffic of military trucks with jeeps full of young, good-looking, jovial soldiers. The uniforms of the American soldiers are neat and youthful, with none of the severity and arrogance of the German uniforms. I notice this right away; what a relief.

The Italians are all out in the streets celebrating the end of five long years of war. It was a cruel war which touched every single person, young and old, and now we cheer the ones who helped to end this war. At last the Americans are here. Jeeps and army trucks are filled with clean, good-looking American soldiers, kissing the beautiful girls. The liberators are here at last. The crowd cheers. Some vehicles stop, the American soldiers try to speak our language. The crowd is happy. They all sing their own songs. Children gather around these young, strong guys, so many of them that I wonder where they come from. Some of the children climb up on the vehicles like monkeys on a tree. The reward is candy, chewing gum, and the like.

A couple of days ago I witnessed hell: gun fire, explosions, nasty screaming. I felt the uncertainty of who was fighting whom. Was the German outpost still around? Were the partisans firing at them or at the fascists, it was difficult to know, to predict the end of it. I hear the cheers, the singing, I see the dancing, embracing, I feel the joy in the fresh April day. I cannot believe the war is over, finished, vanished. I am happy that at last the war is over, and yet at the bottom of my heart I feel sad. I know that my feeling will be different. I feel pain in the pit of my stomach. I try to divert my thoughts and tell myself Mother is fine, she is coming back home soon.

I see a storm of children, ranging from six years old to teenagers, running towards a group of American soldiers. One of the kids is screaming. The Americans are giving away chewy chocolates, even cigarettes. Now the grown-ups start to follow the kids. My head is spinning, so much is going on it is hard to keep calm. At this point my sister and I decide to go back to the house. While we cross the Aurelia in order to reach our house a jeep stops close to us, and the soldiers start greeting us, saying, "Hi baby." My sister looks at me all excited and says, "See, they know my name." They try to stop us and engage in conversation. We smile and keep going on our way home. This is my first encounter with the allied troops.

When we reach home, the afternoon light gently touches the new spring foliage. It is so beautiful and peaceful here. I sit on the shining grass, my sister joins me, and together we enjoy the quiet and beauty of the afternoon. I am exhausted—all that screaming wore me out—and so is my sister. We are lying on the grass and looking up at the blue sky. We both agree that the Americans soldiers are young, clean, and handsome in their military uniforms. "Maybe a little loud," I say. She doesn't agree with me, she thinks they are just wonderful. We both laugh. If only Mother, Daddy, and all the rest of the family were here with us, what a perfect world it would be. Both of us are sitting in silence when we hear Ernesta calling our names. Reluctantly, we get up and go into the house. The sun is no longer shining. The sky is turning pinkish, the sunset is here, and suddenly it is dark.

Once inside the house I look out of the window and see the street lights sparkling. What an amazing sight. For five long years from my windows I could see only darkness and danger. I am fascinated. I keep looking at the gray of the street asphalt shining under the street lights. I feel good and relaxed, no more fear of what might be there in the darkness. The palm trees which stand at the side of the street look majestic with their wide green branches, what a sight. For a long time, I realize now, I have not looked at a palm tree, which is, together with the olive tree, my favorite tree. For five long years the streets all over Italy were pitch black. Whenever I would look at the street in darkness my whole body would ache for fear, feeling the danger. It seemed like death was waiting for the one who would violate the curfew. I still feel the chill. There was no way we could venture out into the night.

From our closed windows I could hear the steps of the German boots hitting the asphalt, echoing in our rooms. We felt fear running in our bones. It is a sound I guess I will never forget and will always associate with danger, fear, and death. There is light out there now to show the way, to lead us into the future. What a joyous feeling, no more anxiety, no more fear of that devilish darkness. No more fear of the future. A euphoric feeling fills the atmosphere around us, which is quite contagious. What is happening right now is quite extraordinary; not even in my wildest dreams could I imagine what has been happening during these last days. It has been a long journey, and now it seems far away. It was not even four days ago that there was fighting in the streets and we were scared. It is hard to believe, but this is the reality. I am happy and yet deep in my heart I am sad. My thoughts are always with Mother. I cannot entirely rejoice in my heart if Mother is not home with us. It hurts deeply.

But I know she is coming back to us soon. Now I concentrate my thoughts and expectations on Mother's return home from the hospital in Savona. The household is busy: cleaning the house, shining the silver, putting flowers all around to welcome Mother back home. It has been such a long time since there was so much activity. Everybody is smiling—I even heard someone singing.

Mother's bedroom upstairs has been freshened up, flowers in the vase on her chest of drawers, windows cleaned and left open in order to let the fresh April breeze come in from the blue Mediterranean Sea. I know tomorrow is going to be the day of Mother's return. I know I am not the only one happy. I see the faces around me; they all look joyous, like living a dream, a wonderful dream.

The door bell rings. It is a soft sound, none the less it takes all of us by surprise. We haven't had a night call for so long we still think in curfew time. Who could be out there? It lasts a split second, and then we realize we are no longer in fear. With no further hesitation on our part we open the door with a big welcome smile.

The night visitor is our friend Franco R. As soon as we see him we rush to greet him affectionately; he is indeed the best friend we have. We make him sit down among us, we want to know above all about Mother; did he speak to the doctors at the hospital? How is she? When is she coming home, when?

"One at a time," Franco pleads. We can see, however, that he is not cross. He knows how eager we are to have news of Mother. We crop around him, anxiously afraid to miss something. Franco smiles while he says, "You will be pleased to know that your mother is coming home tomorrow afternoon." We are all so happy that we cannot utter a single word for a split second, then we all jump around hugging each other. At last we too can celebrate the end of the war, thank God for all you give us. Tomorrow morning we will go to church to thank God and pray for the full recovery of Mother.

At supper we are all over-excited. We talk and laugh like we haven't done for such a long time. It is a spontaneous outburst, a relief from the repressed anxiety which has been inside us for a long time, so long that we do not even remember for how long it has been living in us.

The next morning I wake up early; I certainly do not need anyone to wake me up. The birds are singing, the sun is out in all its splendor. As soon as I open my window the light invades my bedroom and everything is shining. I fix my room as tidily as I can. I must confess I seldom do it, but this morning I am in the right mood. I bathe and wash my hair. I spend a lot of time brushing it carefully. I look for scissors and cut the ends, which do not look even. I look for an outfit which hopefully still fits, not an easy task. I do not own a decent gown; for at least two years I have not bought or made a new outfit. All my clothes are too short and worn out. I try on these old outfits one by one in the hopes of finding a decent one to wear.

I am frustrated and unhappy. At the same time, I am determined to find a decent outfit to greet Mother on her return home. After spending a long time trying on various garments, which now are piling up on my bedroom floor, I would like to be able to show Mother how I changed while she was away. So I decide to change my look. I start with my hairdo, which is the easiest thing to do. I usually part my hair at the side of my forehead, but now I am going to part my hair in the middle. I look in the mirror and approve of what I see. My hair has a fine texture, it gently touches my shoulders, its color is light chestnut, and since I just shampooed and rinsed with white vinegar, it is shining. Often when I walk in the streets of our village I hear the boys saying "Here comes Alida Valli," who happens to be a very popular Italian movie star. I am flattered, but I pretend to be annoyed. I manage to fish out from my closet a navy blue wool skirt which Teresita knitted for us a couple of years ago and which seems to fit, provided I wear it on my hip. I have an old, but in good condition, white blouse that I will wear.

I go to Mother's bedroom to look at myself in her full length mirror. The reflection I see pleases me. Well, I am going to turn fifteen at the end of the month. I really feel good about it. I am happy at the thought that Mother is going to be here to celebrate my birthday with all of us. I am so cheerful that I could kiss everybody, young and old. A warm feeling grabs me; I feel alive like I have never been before.

When I look at myself in the mirror what I see is me of course, and yet I look different. I look different and yet I am my old self, I know it. I keep looking at my reflection in the mirror again and again. Yes it is me and yet I see a different face. I enjoy this game. Lately I have been noticing many young boys older than myself looking at me with a special, unmistakable, admiring and desiring look which makes me feel so wanted and desirable. It is an exhilarating sensation which goes through my whole body from head to toe. What a confusing sensation.

There is one guy at least a couple of years older than myself who lives close to my school. Often I see him standing in front of the school exit door waiting for me.

Every time he approaches me with a smile and says, "Look who is here." Yes, I think, who else? I have to say that this particular guy does trigger my interest. I do not like this guy much. I know he is a nice boy, from a good family, etc., and yet I do not have any feeling about him. I know he has a crush on me, but, honestly my friend I do not care about you. And yet I feel sorry for him. I try to be nice to him, but at the same time I do not want to encourage him too much and try to engage him in conversation.

As I said before, none of all my old clothing fits me anymore. My torso is probably almost the same so the tops fit me just fine, while the skirts are far too short and skimpy. Now all of a sudden I am conscious of my look, of myself. I am uneasy looking at my body. I have no one to confide in with my new concerns. I keep all these sensations to myself and enjoy my little secret.

After the so-called liberation, that is, the end of World War II, we resume our everyday lives. We get up in the morning, have breakfast, skate to school. Life around us is quite different from a few days ago. How can life change so fast? I cannot get over it. People are no longer worried; it is easy to detect it. On the way to school the streets are animated with people going places, greeting each other, exchanging news.

One feels this atmosphere of hope in the future which never existed during the five long years of war, or even before. During classes I see that the students are not paying much attention to the lesson. Another factor strikes me; the teachers smile and do not get upset like they used to. It seems everybody is in a happy, relieved mood. I thank you God for having protected us during the war, and I beg you to send Mother home recovered.

It seems the day is reluctant to come to an end. The darkness is not falling. After school I did my homework, I read my favorite book, Stendhal's *Chartreuse de Parme*. I look out of the window, and the sun is still high in the blue sky. I go to the kitchen to look at the clock, it is five p.m. The sun is still high and bright scarlet beams cross the blue sky. It is so grand, I am fascinated. I indulge, while around me the help, under Ernesta's supervision, are all busy preparing dinner and chatting away. I should go for a walk to the beach while there is still light. If I do, I know the time will go by faster. At the moment I am incapable of making up my mind. I am restless. I get part of a conversation among the kitchen help. "Someone got hold of a fascist hiding in a basement, and he was badly hurt by the communists. It seems he will probably not survive." I quickly get out of the kitchen. I am disgusted, I feel sick to my stomach. I do not want to hear any more about these atrocities. I've had enough of all this bloody useless stuff. We never learn, do we?

At last dinner is served. We all sit down quietly. I know we are all thinking that tomorrow Mother is going to be here with us at last. I am not hungry; I just want the day to be over. Ernesta is urging me to finish my meal. I try to please her, but I cannot, and finally she takes my plate away and replaces it with the fruit salad, which I eat.

At last it is bed time. I rush upstairs, brush my teeth, put my pajamas on and jump into bed and fall asleep. I wake up early in the morning aware of the big day ahead for me, I should say, ahead for us. But it is me I am thinking about. "Are we sure today is the day?" I am wondering, yet I tell myself what Franco told us it would be.

It is a limpid April day, and the sky is of a deep blue. The sea is calm and sparkling under the sun. "What a beautiful day to welcome Mother," I am thinking while going downstairs to breakfast. I am asking Ernesta if everything is ready in Mother's room. She gets a little upset with me, lest I doubt she's doing the right thing. "At what time will Mother and Lalla will be home?" is what everyone is asking. Well, Mother has to check out of the hospital, you know, the usual routine, it takes time, and the trip, well again probably it will be around 11:30. It is nine a.m., so that means two and a half hours to go. I should have gone to school, but then I would not have been able to reach home in time. I am glad I am here to wait, but even so I am restless. I keep going up and down the stairs for no reason at all.

She is here. The gate opens, a car pulls into the driveway, stops, the doors opens and Mother slowly emerges. My heart seems to be jumping out of my white blouse. Here she is. My eyes are watering, tears running down my cheeks. I wipe them off with my hand while I run towards her, as do my siblings. We are all there embracing and kissing her. How many times have I dreamt about this moment!

Mother goes right upstairs to her bedroom to rest after her tip back from the hospital. We follow her upstairs; we are all so eager to be close to her, to be with her, to embrace her . . . to repossess her. I want to stay close to her, to feel her warmth, to smell her, to be with her again. I have missed her so very much. She is pale and fragile, and she has lost weight. It hurts to see her this way. Seeing her like this frightens me. However, her smile, her luminous, unforgettable smile, still lights up her beautiful face and the people around her.

We are sent out of the room. Reluctantly, slowly, we leave Mother's bedroom, looking desperately toward Mother, but inevitably the door shuts. I retreat to my bedroom. I sit on the bed and pick up my favorite book, *The Chartreuse de Parma,* which has been idle for some time. I start reading, but my mind is elsewhere and I am not able to concentrate on my reading. I am not able to follow what I am reading. My thoughts are with Mother. I am worried that she looks so different, so gray. It hurts so much. I try to convince myself that now that she is home we will take good care of her. "I am sure she is going to recoup fast, I am sure of it," I keep saying to myself.

Mother does not come down to dine with us. Instead her meal is served in her bedroom. She is too tired, we have been informed. We are all very quiet. No one feels like talking. For my part I do not feel like eating either. At last dinner is over. We eat our fruit, but do not go out like we have been doing lately because the evenings at the end of April are extremely pleasant. The evenings right now are peacefully beautiful. I enjoy going out in the early evening when the sunset's light still lingers, the blue sky becomes pink, and it suddenly turns into a dark violet color. What a sight; it does not last long but it is magic. I love it. I only wish it would last a little longer. Tonight, however, I do not feel like going out for my evening walk. I want to stay close to Mother. As soon as the dinner table is cleared of all the plates, we gather around the table to play a card game. I am not paying attention to the game, and my partner, my sister Baby, is furious. She keeps looking at me, imploring me to pay attention, but it seems I am not able to do so. I quit among a roar of disapproval.

I go upstairs by Mother's bedroom. There is no light filtering through the closed door. She is probably reading using her bedside lamp. I am tempted to knock, but I decide not to because she may be sleeping, and I would feel really badly if I woke her up. She needs a lot of rest to be able to recover fully, the doctor told us.

Once in my room I jump on my bed and get hold of one of my school books. I throw it back where it came from. I go to the bathroom to brush my teeth. It is such a pleasure to brush my teeth now, since we are able to buy good toothpaste. During the war it was really difficult to find that stuff. My sister joins me but does not say a word, starts undressing, and goes to bed. I turn the light off and go to bed too.

In the morning I wake up earlier than usual in order to

have time to go to visit with Mother before breakfast and then off to school. Mother has just woken up, and her breakfast tray is in front of her. She looks better than the day of her arrival from the hospital. I am happy and relieved. I want to hug and kiss her, but instead I just look at her. She smiles and I am so happy. Everybody is crowding the room to say good morning to Mother before going to school.

School days are different than just a couple of months ago. Both the teachers as well as the students are not focusing on their work. I am trying to figure out the cause of this behavior. Is it the spring air coming in from the classroom's open window? Or is everybody dreaming about the new free world in front of us? Anyway, when the dismissing bell rings the classroom is empty in a second. My sister and I leave school as fast as possible like everybody else. The village's streets are crowded with pedestrians, bicycles, and horse-driven carts full of merchandise like I have never seen. Even before the war I do not remember all this traffic; it has always been a sleepy village, now it is bursting with activity.

At home we rush to Mother's bedroom. She is in the armchair wearing a purple velvet robe with a cream collar. Our sister Lalla is painting her portrait, and we know she doesn't like interruption while she paints. We immediately stop at the door. Mother sees us and says, "Come in, girls." One by one we approach her and embrace. Mother enquires about our studies, about our teachers and friends. We all talk together and soon we have to leave the room as Mother is visibly tired. We are happy to have her home. We want her to revive and be like she was. I go to my room, and here alone I pray God to make Mother recover fully.

Days go by. We go to school, come back home, do our homework, and play with our friends, trying to lead a normal life. Mother is better, but she is not allowed to leave her room as yet. This hurts me a lot. One day we come home from school and the staff is busy packing all of our belonging. We are going back to live in our house. What great news! At last we can move back to our home. By night I am home, in my bedroom, in my bed. It feels so good to be home again. I look around; it's just like we left it a couple of years ago. Good, I am happy and so is everybody else in our family. I can see in their faces, and everybody is smiling. Well it seems those five long years of war are over and gone. What a difference from when we last lived here, the German troops living next door, the curfew, the night raids.

Now I am lying in my bed. I get up, open the window, and look outside. The night is dark, but what a reassuring silence, broken only by the perpetual sound of the sea waves hitting the shore. Reassured, I close the window shutter and go back to my comfortable bed.

I wake up in the morning to the sound of hammering. I am wondering what the sound is. I open the window and see a couple of men erecting wooden cabanas on the beach in front of us. "Do you know what this means?" I'm asking myself. It means we are back to normalcy. I jump out of bed, wake up my sister, and run to the kitchen to break the news. To my disappointment, no one really cares. I think they do not understand the meaning of the cabanas. It means we are looking to our future with confidence. I am happy.

It is the end of the school year. The sweet smell of summer is in the air. The Mediterranean Sea is cobalt blue; it looks like a postcard. We all pass with flying colors. We put away our school paraphernalia. May goes by fast. June, with its sunny days and balmy nights, goes even faster. We seldom are allowed in Mother's bedroom. We spend our days at the beach with our peers. Many families who own villas and apartments are back in town after so many years of not being able to vacation. In town the movie theaters are opening, to our great happiness. Of course my favorite movie theater is the outdoor one. It is located in a beautiful garden. My only complaint is that the chairs are not so comfortable. No problem, we carry our own cushions to protect our honorable rear ends. We also carry a woolen shawl; in the evening it gets damp and chilly.

If only I could I would go every single night and attend every show. I would probably be the happiest girl alive. I adore sitting in the dark watching these amazing movies. The movie soundtrack at night is pure magic. Not even in my wild imagination could I ever be able to recreate what I see. I am captured by all the images of these handsome actors and actresses. I am enchanted. When the movie is over I do not want to go home. I want to see more, more.

The day after we discuss with our friends what we saw at the movies the night before. It seems that every one of us has seen the same movie, but each one of us got a different angle of it. I myself find it fascinating what a great communication and entertainment tool it is.

Anyway, what I would like to do is one thing, and what I am allowed to do is another. So, we go to the movies once a week, and the movie feature has to be approved by the grown-ups of course. At first we kids are not so happy about this, but then we think it is much better than not going to the movies at all.

We make new friends, boys and girls. I should feel good about myself for a couple of reasons. First, I am very popular among the boys. I am a good swimmer. I am not afraid to dive from the highest rock. No other girl is capable of doing so. Also I am good at volleyball and the only girl on the team. And yet, I am not happy. I am worried about Mother's health. It is something I carry with me. My thoughts are always with her.

We kids start our day quite early in the morning. After breakfast we go to the beach which is practically deserted, and the life guards are cleaning the sand and fixing their sun umbrellas. It is probably the best time of the day at the beach. It is quiet, almost deserted, and we own the place.

I wish Mother could join us to enjoy these peaceful mornings. Unfortunately we do not see any improvement in Mother's health. This hurts me badly; it is hard to see your own mother, the person you love most in the whole world, suffering so much. I pray to God night and day asking him to help Mother recover. I promise to be good, obedient, devoted, anything . . .

I have been noticing lately that Mother's doctor comes to the house more frequently, sometimes twice a day, and this worries me very much. The doctor takes longer to complete his examination. I know for a fact that the doctor respects Mother's judgment and often consults with her on various matters. This is my great and only hope. When the doctor leaves Mother's bedroom, if it happens that I cross him in the hall he doesn't look at me; he bends his head slightly and keeps going on his way. I freeze. I want to ask him many questions, but by the time I formulate my words he is gone out the front door. I want to run after him, but I don't move, I see the door closing. I am upset and angry and feel like insulting him. "Idiot," I say in sotto voce.

If I think about it, it is not the first time this has happened. The last time the doctor behaved this way I thought maybe he was late for his next patient. But now I have my doubts. I try to make believe that it is not happening, that it is just not happening. For a little while I believe it.

Why did we survive the war, the air raids, the German occupation, and all those terrible things, and now that is over,

Mother is not well? Is this fair? I am upset and cannot understand what is going on. I try to sneak into Mother's bedroom, but there is always someone who grabs me and sends me out of the room, to my great disappointment.

I busy myself making order in my chest of drawers or my closet. At this point I do not own much of anything. We have not been shopping for clothing lately. I sort my clothing, keeping what fits and making an orderly pile of the stuff I want to get rid of. It feels good to see how neat my drawers are. I keep opening them to enjoy what I have done. The white blouses are neatly folded, then in the next drawer the colored ones, then in the third drawer all the underwear and the nightgowns. I wonder why I waited such a long time to do all this cleaning up of all this old faded clothing. I am sure if Mother knows she is going to be proud of me. As a matter of fact, I am trying to keep myself as busy as possible. I look around and everything looks great. I open the drawers one by one, beaming with pleasure that everything in my bedroom is in good order. Satisfied, I gather the discarded stuff and take it to the kitchen. Sure enough, Ernesta is presiding over the kitchen staff, and she assures me that she knows someone who will be able to use the stuff. So I leave the kitchen with a feeling of having accomplishing something good.

Indeed right now the weather is spectacular: an ideal temperature, coldish during the morning and night but warm and dry during the day. If only Mother could enjoy it I would be the happiest human being alive!

Chapter 18

The early summer months go by uneventfully. Mother's health is not improving as desired, which saddens me. I feel disappointed and bitter towards the world surrounding me. The war, with all its hardship, has been over for a while. I am not able to celebrate it. There is no joy in my heart. Why, I am asking myself, is Mother sick? I wish I could be sick instead of her. We are a free country, free to do what we please, free to say what we want. Frankly I do not care. I really do not care, I keep telling myself. What is all the fuss about? So many people have been killed in the war, military as well as innocent civilians, but no one talks about this. Do you call it fair? I really do not understand, and it hurts. That is why I cannot rejoice with my countrymen. I know freedom is important for a nation and its citizens, but is it worth the killing of all these poor victims? Is it? Does anyone understand my point? I have my doubts.

When I look around what do I see but people busy minding their own interests. This is probably what democracy is all about. What do I know? I have never lived in a Democratic country. I know as well that it is not me talking, but my bitterness.

One morning, as soon as I wake up, I sense something unusual is happening.

Sure enough, we are told that Mother is going to Milan to be admitted to the hospital. I am aware of Mother's poor health at this point, but it is hard for me to acknowledge it. I am enraged; I feel betrayed by the whole world. I feel helpless and lonely. When the car arrives to pick up Mother and my sister Lalla to be driven to Milan to the hospital, it comes as a shock. I know Mother is going, but when they show up I am shocked. I know it is happening in front of us, but I am refusing to acknowledge it. I see Mother approaching the vehicle. We all gather around her as she kisses us one by one. When she kisses me I detect right away the delicate perfume of her Chanel No. 5. I like it so much. I want to hold her face close to mine, but she gets into the car.

The car door closes, and the car at first goes slowly, then it takes off fast and suddenly is no longer in sight. An unbearable void is hitting my stomach. I want to call Mother. No sound is coming out from my dried mouth. We all stand looking at the empty road in front of us. I feel tears running down my cheeks. We all stand there in silence, unable to make a move. After a while, which to me seems an eternity, we all walk back into the house.

As soon as I get to the house, which seems awfully empty,

I take refuge in my bedroom. It is the end of the month of July, and the sun is strong even during the mornings. When she is finished tidying up the rooms in the mornings, the maid makes sure all the wooden shutters outside are closed tight, to keep it cool during the hot days. I must say it does work. The room is cool and awfully depressing. I lay on my bed crying, unable to stop my sobbing. I guess I fall asleep.

Not having any notion of how long I have been lying there, I open my tired eyes and see the sunlight filtered through the closed shutters. It must be midday. I do not have any desire to eat or see anybody, however I manage to get up and venture out of my bedroom.

To my great surprise everything is exactly as it was before. I direct myself toward the kitchen. I glance inside; everybody is busy preparing lunch. I cannot understand how anyone can possibly be able to eat at a time like this. The thought of eating makes me sick to my stomach. I am going back to my bedroom to nurture my desperation. I want to be alone, to think about Mother, to be with her, to see her warm, beautiful smile, her warm embrace . . . "God," I pray, "help Mother to recuperate. I want her back with us." I pray in the darkness of my room. It seems to me I will never recover or get over my sorrows.

A couple of days after Mother's departure Aunt Gabriella arrives at the house followed by a load of luggage. She is here to look after us, I guess. In any other circumstances I would be delighted to have Aunt Gabriella staying with us. But now it is hard for me to accept her presence in the house. First of all, she smokes far too much, and I cannot stand the cigarette smell. She even smokes in Mother's room, which she is occupying at present. Aunt Gabriella, as everybody knows, reads and smokes all night long. I used to find it very "*a la page*," but now I find it dreadful. I am furious. How can she smoke in Mother's bedroom?

To be fair, Aunt Gabriella is trying hard to be kind to all of us. She takes us to the outdoor movies since she knows we all love it. The garden where the movie theatre is located is surrounded by tall African palms. A strong scent of jasmine permeates the air around us. What a wonderful treat to sit here looking up at the sky shining with a myriad of beaming stars. It is simply magic to me even if the feature presentation is not as good as the setting. It is worth the ticket price.

Often Aunt Gabriella treats us and our friends to the outdoor café for ice cream. We all love to sit at the café watching people go by and be seen. The war has been over for no more than three months, and no one seems to remember it. Few people talk about it; everybody seems busy doing whatever they do. My countrymen, the Italians, seem busy reconstructing their lives, their houses and cities. The freedom won has opened new horizons never before possible. The newspapers report the birth of new political parties, so many of them it is impossible to remember them all. I am not into politics, but my curiosity is such that it makes me try hard to keep up with events.

The Communist and the Christian Democrat parties seem to be the ones which have the most followers, and indeed they fight verbally in their newspapers, and often in the squares they fist-fight and more. So now the big battle is mostly between these two parties. Of course they both claim to be the only one which could lead us to becoming a modern democratic nation. The newspapers report daily of gatherings in the squares of the big cities around the country, often with fights between the Communists and Christian democrats. In one year's time free elections will be held in our country. I am too young to be able to cast my vote, but all the same I am excited. What a wonderful thing to be able to participate in as a country, how civilized.

We are lucky, in our village people do not have time to demonstrate in the square. They all seem busy reconstructing their lives, their houses, and their businesses. The national newspapers are commenting on all these new freedom movements. Sometimes I am very confused; so much is happening I cannot very often grasp it all. I go on with my daily life.

Lately I have been noticing that boys are looking at me with, what can I say, interest to say the least. They gather around me trying to get my attention. I am enjoying this new development in my social life; it is certainly a new experience. I might be vain, but it feels awfully good inside. I must admit at school I have been popular among my classmates, but those were girls. These are the male counterpart. Another factor which influences my social popularity is the fact that I am good at sports. When the kids are getting together a team for a volleyball game, I am always on their list. Mind you, I am the only female on the team.

All these diversions fill my summer days at the beach, but my thoughts are constantly with Mother, as if I have a thorn in my heart I miss her so much. Mother is still at the hospital in Milan, we have been told. No one really keeps us up to date on her condition, and thus it is difficult to live with. I honestly wish they would tell us more details about Mother. It is painful. I am sad, unhappy, and restless. I wish I could go to her and stay with her. I dream sometimes of being with her, nursing Mother day and night. Very often I do not know if I am dreaming or if it is really happening, my desire to be with Mother is so very deep.

Aunt Gabriella is still smoking away night and day. This is what annoys me the most lately. I am trying to be reasonable. I try to be polite and kind and understanding towards Aunty. I know she is aware of my present feeling towards her. She knows I constantly compare her with Mother, her sister. I have to admit that she tries her best to entertain us by telling us about the book she is reading, succeeding in capturing our devoted attention. She amuses us with her strong sense of humor and her captivating smile, which reminds me of Mother's.

Our life goes on in the hopes of soon receiving good news

about Mother. We miss her so very much: her radiant, reassuring smile, her warm bosom. It is a hot, sunny, lazy summer afternoon. We had a late lunch because of our lateness returning from the beach. Aunt Gabriella, who hates delayed lunches, scolds us severely. My hair is still wet and salty, dripping on the immaculate white table cloth. All this upsets Ernesta, who is serving lunch. She and the rest of the kitchen crew are late for their afternoon siesta. She darts her eyes around the table. Her look reminds me of "*Caron Demonio con occhi di bragia*," a quote that you can find in Dante's *Inferno*, which translates into "Chadron the Demon with charcoal eyes." (Canto III, "The Gate of Hell.") So we keep quiet, heads down on our dishes, trying to be proper in order not to aggravate the already tense situation.

Finally lunch is over and we are dismissed while our aunt remains in the dining room with her cigarettes and newspapers. We retreat to our bedrooms for our siesta. I comb my now-dry hair and lay on my bed. The curtains are drawn, and the sea breeze makes them hit the window frame with a constant sound similar to waves. It is a lovely lullaby, and I gently fall asleep, as does my sister.

I have been playing volleyball all morning with the boys at the beach. I am the only girl on the all-boy team. I am fast and I learned to serve well, so I am in demand. I do not make a fuss if one of the boys hits me hard while we're playing. I go on playing. I am most admired for that, as well as appreciated.

At the beginning of August the days are sunny, hot, and lazy. A little breeze gently caresses the top of the deep blue Mediterranean Sea like a sudden electric wave. A sense of torpor lingers in the air in August's lazy days. At night it is warmish. The crickets sing their monotonous song, and I wish it would never stop. I love the summer nights when the sky is dark but lit up by those beautiful, mysterious stars. You feel the universe alive, pulsing away. I am never tired of looking up at the stars; they are so amazing in their brightness. I am impressed by God's creativity. I am moved by this spectacular sight which takes my breath away.

I feel like a little dot, and yet I feel good to be able to be here to enjoy it.

We are often scolded for coming home late from our evening strolls with our friends. How can I possibly explain to Aunt Gabriella how much we enjoy the tender August nights with those millions of stars beaming on top of us? I feel the greatness and the mystery of the universe. The more I look up at the sky, the more I feel like a little dot. I wonder why we do not spend more time looking at the stars instead of going to sleep or staying inside the house.

One morning we are chatting away at the breakfast table when Aunt Gabriella suddenly appears at the door. She is standing there to our great surprise; we usually do not see her before lunchtime. She is still wearing her laced negligee, her hair not properly combed. Looking at her my heart stops beating. I know right away something terrible has happened. Aunt Gabriella's eyes are red, her lips are trembling, and she is trying to speak. "Your mother . . . last night." She cannot utter another word. We all look at each other in despair and start crying. As soon as I am able to control my crying, I run out of the kitchen to my bedroom. "It is not true, it cannot be true," I keep saying over and over again while crying uncontrollably.

I sit in the only armchair in the room. I am overwhelmed by this terrible, unbearable event. I am mad at everybody. Why Mother? Why? It is not happening; it cannot be true. I just cannot reconcile or accept this cruel loss. I cannot stop crying. I feel like punishing myself. I hit my head against the white wall of the room. I do not know what I am doing.

Exhausted, I lay down on my bed. My head hurts badly. "God please help me, this is not happening. It is just a nightmare. It is not happening." Suddenly my eyes are dried out; no more tears are coming down my cheeks. A violent rage is building up in my entire body. I am shaking, unable to control it. Finally I lay down in my bed, motionless. A soft knock at the door wakes me from my torpor. I do not have any idea of the time. I know, however, that I am not in a mood to see or talk to anyone. I close my tired eyes again and lay on the bed, motionless.

I hear familiar sounds: whispers, the hurried steps of someone passing in the hall. I feel empty. I feel defenseless, like an orphan. I want to fall asleep and never wake up again . . .

But the next morning I wake up as usual when the violent August sun, in spite of the heavy wooden shutters, comes in. A strong smell of coffee invades the room as well. It is breakfast time. My eyes are wide open, and it feels like waking up from an illness. My body and mind are light. I look around the room as if I am in a strange place . . . but everything is where it belongs. The big old mirror hangs on the wall. My sister's bed is here close to mine, even though right now it is empty. Probably she is at breakfast. My sorrow and desperation of yesterday have been replaced by a peaceful mood. I am grateful, and I thank God for it in my morning prayers.

I get up from bed and, in my pajamas, join the family at breakfast. Aunt Gabriella looks pretty and put together. It is unusual to see her so early in the morning, but we are going to attend the Holy Mass for Mother at the Benedettini convent in Finalpia. I look around the table; my sister Baby is drinking her *caffe e latte* holding the cup with both hands, staring at the wall. She looks perhaps a little older, more grown up, it seems to me. Mario looks the same, well behaved like a little gentleman. I smile, and he smiles back.

Ernesta tells my sister and me that she has pressed the white dresses we have to wear for church. She will bring them to our bedroom in order for us to put them on. My sister Baby and I go back to our quarters to get ready for the mass. We get dressed, but I cannot find my black veil to put on my head. I look everywhere, in all the drawers, then under a pile of tops I see it, with much relief! My sister gets hold of it and shouts, "This is mine, do not dare wear it!" We almost start a quarrel when Ernesta comes in the room holding a black veil in her hand.

When it is time to go to church, we all walk together. The church is not that far away from our house, probably half a mile. Many friends gather around us after the function. I am grateful that they just hug me. No speeches, otherwise I would break into tears. I hate to show my emotions in public.

Lunch after church is quiet, but not sad. It seems that all of us feel closer to each other like never before. This fills my heart with joy.

We stay mostly at home these days. I busy myself reading whatever book I find. The other kids mostly play card games. I hear their voices. I think our friend next door, Pilin, has joined them to play cards or maybe some other games. Late in the afternoon our friend Renata shows up. I am pleased to see her. We girls decide to go to the beach.

So we go and sit on the chaise lounge chatting while the afternoon is fading away. The only people around us are the two lifeguards busy closing the blue umbrellas and combing the sand. When their job is finished they sit with us. We talk and watch the sun vanishing into the blue Mediterranean Sea. The conversation stops as we all are taken by this beautiful sight. I feel peaceful. We indulge for a while, then we go back home.

A week goes by, and one day we learn that Daddy and our eldest sister Lalla are going to spend the remainder of the summer with us. They arrive, and we cheer. We are a reunited family again. This is such a comfortable feeling. Daddy is still handsome, his hair is almost all white, his brownish almond eyes have not lost their sparkle. I have forgotten how much I love him.

I thought Aunt Gabriella was strict, but Daddy is much more so. Lunch hour has to be respected, no excuses accepted. After a while we all get used to it. We make Daddy happy. He likes to eat at exactly one p.m. If we want to eat lunch we better be on time. One of his favorite dishes is a fish called *branzino*. He likes it with boiled potatoes, homemade mayonnaise, and local white wine. The fish are caught in loco, and they are special indeed. I enjoy this dish very much, and we kids are allowed to taste the wine. It is cool and goes down smoothly . . . I love it.

After lunch, when it is really hot, my sister Baby and I go to our room for a nap. There is something special about a hot August afternoon, everything still and so quiet.

The month of August is swept away by violent storms. My father keeps saying, "The first storms mark the end of summer." I do not like to hear that at all. Sure enough the calm Mediterranean is swelling with gigantic waves and the wind as well is very strong. The beach already looks like the fall. The sun umbrellas have been removed, the boats moved up far away from the shore. A crowd is watching this beautiful happening! A red flag is flying on a pole, meaning no one is allowed to go in the water. The only ones braving the fearful waves are the two lifeguards.

I am standing with many others watching the two guys. I envy them, wishing I could join them . . . what a challenge it would be! One of them gets out, comes close to me, and grabs my arm shouting, "Come on in!" With no hesitation I dive into the high waves coming towards me with an unbelievable violence. It gets hold of my body, flips it up, and I feel like a puppet at the mercy of the ocean. When I come out of the first wave immediately another big wave comes towards me; I dive in again and again. I barely have time to get air in my lungs when I have to dive again.

After a while I feel it is time to try to get to shore. I know that the only way to accomplish that is to stay on top of the wave, letting myself go with the current. So I close my eyes and do it—I let myself go. The strong wave turns into a whirlpool. I am in the middle of it. I am trapped. I do not know what is happening. I am underwater. I feel sand mixed with gravel hitting my body, my head. Everything is happening fast. Eventually I find myself catapulted to shore at the feet of the watching crowd. I am shaken up but all right I guess.

When I get up, my swimming suit almost falls down, there are so many pebbles in it. I am embarrassed and try to pull the swimming suit up. The crowd is applauding. I feel good. Baby is following me while I am going to the cabana to dry up and get dressed. She keeps saying, "Were you scared, were you?"

"Well, actually I didn't have any time to be scared, everything happened so fast. The waves never stop . . . it is perpetual motion!"

At dinner when Daddy hears the event of the day my glory has a short life. "It was indeed very silly," Daddy says, "for a young girl to do such a dangerous thing." I am tempted to respond to this that the lifeguards trusted my skills, why doesn't he? But I do not dare. I don't utter a word in my defense.

The days are getting shorter. Often strong winds coming from the east blow away whatever is around. The days are clear, and the sun is bright. "It seems September weather already," I hear someone say, and I must agree. We kids still go to the beach, which is now deserted. We place ourselves between the wooden boats called *gozzi*. Here we are protected from the strong wind.

It is time for the family to go back to Milan to resume our normal life. When I first hear this news, I feel a little bit of hesitation. We have been here for five years. We went through rough times and happy times too, and it is not easy to let it all go. But all things considered, I am ready to go to my native place.

It is early morning when we start our journey back to

Milan. The sun is young but already shining in the blue morning sky. Before leaving my bedroom I glance at myself in the wall mirror. I smile, pleased with what I see. The via Aurelia is empty of cars, buses, or any other vehicle. I am rested, full of energy, and eager to leave. We do not have a lot of stuff to bring to the city, and we are using a Fiat 500 called Topolino. It is a very small car with a great engine and a big heart. This particular car is pre-war but still going strong. Of course it has been idle for five years, hidden in a stable. I am amazed that it does not stink.

We all fit in, with my sister Gabriella and me sitting in the front seat next to the driver. Ernesta and Mario Jr. are in the back seat. The trip though the winding road along the coast goes through beautiful villages. It is a five hour drive from Finalpia to Milan. After two and a half hours we reach Genoa, where we stop for lunch.

In spite of the uncomfortable seating arrangements, I am enjoying the trip. As we approach the city, the traffic gets more intense with buses, motorcycles making a lot of noise, and trucks loaded to capacity keeping us busy looking at them. As soon as the car stops at the parking lot, my sister and I jump out immediately. I am stiff as hell; I stretch my aching limbs like a cat waking up after having slept all day on a couch.

We are astonished by the animated scene in front of us. The Genoa Harbor. My sister and I hold hands and smile. It is the brave new world in front of us. We are part of it!

www.ingramcontent.com/pod-product-compliance
Lightning Source LLC
Chambersburg PA
CBHW030320080526
44584CB00012B/643